GNU GRUB Reference Manual

A catalogue record for this book is available from the Hong Kong Public Libraries.

Published in Hong Kong by Samurai Media Limited.

Email: info@samuraimedia.org

ISBN 978-988-8381-84-5

Background Cover Image by https://www.flickr.com/people/webtreatsetc/

Table of Contents

1 Introduction to GRUB

1.1 Overview

Briefly, a *boot loader* is the first software program that runs when a computer starts. It is responsible for loading and transferring control to an operating system *kernel* software (such as Linux or GNU Mach). The kernel, in turn, initializes the rest of the operating system (e.g. a GNU system).

GNU GRUB is a very powerful boot loader, which can load a wide variety of free operating systems, as well as proprietary operating systems with chain-loading[1]. GRUB is designed to address the complexity of booting a personal computer; both the program and this manual are tightly bound to that computer platform, although porting to other platforms may be addressed in the future.

One of the important features in GRUB is flexibility; GRUB understands filesystems and kernel executable formats, so you can load an arbitrary operating system the way you like, without recording the physical position of your kernel on the disk. Thus you can load the kernel just by specifying its file name and the drive and partition where the kernel resides.

When booting with GRUB, you can use either a command-line interface (see Section 12.1 [Command-line interface], page 45), or a menu interface (see Section 12.2 [Menu interface], page 46). Using the command-line interface, you type the drive specification and file name of the kernel manually. In the menu interface, you just select an OS using the arrow keys. The menu is based on a configuration file which you prepare beforehand (see Chapter 5 [Configuration], page 17). While in the menu, you can switch to the command-line mode, and vice-versa. You can even edit menu entries before using them.

In the following chapters, you will learn how to specify a drive, a partition, and a file name (see Chapter 2 [Naming convention], page 7) to GRUB, how to install GRUB on your drive (see Chapter 3 [Installation], page 9), and how to boot your OSes (see Chapter 4 [Booting], page 13), step by step.

1.2 History of GRUB

GRUB originated in 1995 when Erich Boleyn was trying to boot the GNU Hurd with the University of Utah's Mach 4 microkernel (now known as GNU Mach). Erich and Brian Ford designed the Multiboot Specification (see Section "Motivation" in *The Multiboot Specification*), because they were determined not to add to the large number of mutually-incompatible PC boot methods.

Erich then began modifying the FreeBSD boot loader so that it would understand Multiboot. He soon realized that it would be a lot easier to write his own boot loader from scratch than to keep working on the FreeBSD boot loader, and so GRUB was born.

Erich added many features to GRUB, but other priorities prevented him from keeping up with the demands of its quickly-expanding user base. In 1999, Gordon Matzigkeit and

---

[1] *chain-load* is the mechanism for loading unsupported operating systems by loading another boot loader. It is typically used for loading DOS or Windows.

Yoshinori K. Okuji adopted GRUB as an official GNU package, and opened its development by making the latest sources available via anonymous CVS. See Appendix A [Obtaining and Building GRUB], page 107, for more information.

Over the next few years, GRUB was extended to meet many needs, but it quickly became clear that its design was not keeping up with the extensions being made to it, and we reached the point where it was very difficult to make any further changes without breaking existing features. Around 2002, Yoshinori K. Okuji started work on PUPA (Preliminary Universal Programming Architecture for GNU GRUB), aiming to rewrite the core of GRUB to make it cleaner, safer, more robust, and more powerful. PUPA was eventually renamed to GRUB 2, and the original version of GRUB was renamed to GRUB Legacy. Small amounts of maintenance continued to be done on GRUB Legacy, but the last release (0.97) was made in 2005 and at the time of writing it seems unlikely that there will be another.

By around 2007, GNU/Linux distributions started to use GRUB 2 to limited extents, and by the end of 2009 multiple major distributions were installing it by default.

1.3 Differences from previous versions

GRUB 2 is a rewrite of GRUB (see Section 1.2 [History], page 1), although it shares many characteristics with the previous version, now known as GRUB Legacy. Users of GRUB Legacy may need some guidance to find their way around this new version.

- The configuration file has a new name ('grub.cfg' rather than 'menu.lst' or 'grub.conf'), new syntax (see Chapter 5 [Configuration], page 17) and many new commands (see Chapter 14 [Commands], page 53). Configuration cannot be copied over directly, although most GRUB Legacy users should not find the syntax too surprising.

- 'grub.cfg' is typically automatically generated by grub-mkconfig (see Section 5.1 [Simple configuration], page 17). This makes it easier to handle versioned kernel upgrades.

- Partition numbers in GRUB device names now start at 1, not 0 (see Chapter 2 [Naming convention], page 7).

- The configuration file is now written in something closer to a full scripting language: variables, conditionals, and loops are available.

- A small amount of persistent storage is available across reboots, using the save_env and load_env commands in GRUB and the grub-editenv utility. This is not available in all configurations (see Section 13.2 [Environment block], page 51).

- GRUB 2 has more reliable ways to find its own files and those of target kernels on multiple-disk systems, and has commands (see Section 14.3.40 [search], page 63) to find devices using file system labels or Universally Unique Identifiers (UUIDs).

- GRUB 2 is available for several other types of system in addition to the PC BIOS systems supported by GRUB Legacy: PC EFI, PC coreboot, PowerPC, SPARC, and MIPS Lemote Yeeloong are all supported.

- Many more file systems are supported, including but not limited to ext4, HFS+, and NTFS.

- GRUB 2 can read files directly from LVM and RAID devices.

- A graphical terminal and a graphical menu system are available.

- GRUB 2's interface can be translated, including menu entry names.
- The image files (see Chapter 10 [Images], page 41) that make up GRUB have been reorganised; Stage 1, Stage 1.5, and Stage 2 are no more.
- GRUB 2 puts many facilities in dynamically loaded modules, allowing the core image to be smaller, and allowing the core image to be built in more flexible ways.

1.4 GRUB features

The primary requirement for GRUB is that it be compliant with the *Multiboot Specification*, which is described in Section "Motivation" in *The Multiboot Specification*.

The other goals, listed in approximate order of importance, are:

- Basic functions must be straightforward for end-users.
- Rich functionality to support kernel experts and designers.
- Backward compatibility for booting FreeBSD, NetBSD, OpenBSD, and Linux. Proprietary kernels (such as DOS, Windows NT, and OS/2) are supported via a chain-loading function.

Except for specific compatibility modes (chain-loading and the Linux *piggyback* format), all kernels will be started in much the same state as in the Multiboot Specification. Only kernels loaded at 1 megabyte or above are presently supported. Any attempt to load below that boundary will simply result in immediate failure and an error message reporting the problem.

In addition to the requirements above, GRUB has the following features (note that the Multiboot Specification doesn't require all the features that GRUB supports):

Recognize multiple executable formats
> Support many of the *a.out* variants plus *ELF*. Symbol tables are also loaded.

Support non-Multiboot kernels
> Support many of the various free 32-bit kernels that lack Multiboot compliance (primarily FreeBSD, NetBSD, OpenBSD, and Linux). Chain-loading of other boot loaders is also supported.

Load multiples modules
> Fully support the Multiboot feature of loading multiple modules.

Load a configuration file
> Support a human-readable text configuration file with preset boot commands. You can also load another configuration file dynamically and embed a preset configuration file in a GRUB image file. The list of commands (see Chapter 14 [Commands], page 53) are a superset of those supported on the command-line. An example configuration file is provided in Chapter 5 [Configuration], page 17.

Provide a menu interface
> A menu interface listing preset boot commands, with a programmable timeout, is available. There is no fixed limit on the number of boot entries, and the current implementation has space for several hundred.

Have a flexible command-line interface

> A fairly flexible command-line interface, accessible from the menu, is available to edit any preset commands, or write a new boot command set from scratch. If no configuration file is present, GRUB drops to the command-line.

> The list of commands (see Chapter 14 [Commands], page 53) are a subset of those supported for configuration files. Editing commands closely resembles the Bash command-line (see Section 12.1 [Command-line interface], page 45), with TAB-completion of commands, devices, partitions, and files in a directory depending on context.

Support multiple filesystem types

> Support multiple filesystem types transparently, plus a useful explicit blocklist notation. The currently supported filesystem types are *Amiga Fast FileSystem (AFFS)*, *AtheOS fs*, *BeFS*, *BtrFS* (including raid0, raid1, raid10, gzip and lzo), *cpio* (little- and big-endian bin, odc and newc variants), *Linux ext2/ext3/ext4*, *DOS FAT12/FAT16/FAT32*, *exFAT*, *HFS*, *HFS+*, *ISO9660* (including Joliet, Rock-ridge and multi-chunk files), *JFS*, *Minix fs* (versions 1, 2 and 3), *nilfs2*, *NTFS* (including compression), *ReiserFS*, *ROMFS*, *Amiga Smart FileSystem (SFS)*, *Squash4*, *tar*, *UDF*, *BSD UFS/UFS2*, *XFS*, and *ZFS* (including lzjb, gzip, zle, mirror, stripe, raidz1/2/3 and encryption in AES-CCM and AES-GCM). See Chapter 11 [Filesystem], page 43, for more information.

Support automatic decompression

> Can decompress files which were compressed by `gzip` or `xz`[2]. This function is both automatic and transparent to the user (i.e. all functions operate upon the uncompressed contents of the specified files). This greatly reduces a file size and loading time, a particularly great benefit for floppies.[3]

> It is conceivable that some kernel modules should be loaded in a compressed state, so a different module-loading command can be specified to avoid uncompressing the modules.

Access data on any installed device

> Support reading data from any or all floppies or hard disk(s) recognized by the BIOS, independent of the setting of the root device.

Be independent of drive geometry translations

> Unlike many other boot loaders, GRUB makes the particular drive translation irrelevant. A drive installed and running with one translation may be converted to another translation without any adverse effects or changes in GRUB's configuration.

Detect all installed RAM

> GRUB can generally find all the installed RAM on a PC-compatible machine. It uses an advanced BIOS query technique for finding all memory regions. As described on the Multiboot Specification (see Section "Motivation" in *The Multi-*

---

[2] Only CRC32 data integrity check is supported (xz default is CRC64 so one should use –check=crc32 option). LZMA BCJ filters are supported.

[3] There are a few pathological cases where loading a very badly organized ELF kernel might take longer, but in practice this never happen.

boot Specification), not all kernels make use of this information, but GRUB provides it for those who do.

Support Logical Block Address mode

In traditional disk calls (called *CHS mode*), there is a geometry translation problem, that is, the BIOS cannot access over 1024 cylinders, so the accessible space is limited to at least 508 MB and to at most 8GB. GRUB can't universally solve this problem, as there is no standard interface used in all machines. However, several newer machines have the new interface, Logical Block Address (*LBA*) mode. GRUB automatically detects if LBA mode is available and uses it if available. In LBA mode, GRUB can access the entire disk.

Support network booting

GRUB is basically a disk-based boot loader but also has network support. You can load OS images from a network by using the *TFTP* protocol.

Support remote terminals

To support computers with no console, GRUB provides remote terminal support, so that you can control GRUB from a remote host. Only serial terminal support is implemented at the moment.

1.5 The role of a boot loader

The following is a quotation from Gordon Matzigkeit, a GRUB fanatic:

Some people like to acknowledge both the operating system and kernel when they talk about their computers, so they might say they use "GNU/Linux" or "GNU/Hurd". Other people seem to think that the kernel is the most important part of the system, so they like to call their GNU operating systems "Linux systems."

I, personally, believe that this is a grave injustice, because the *boot loader* is the most important software of all. I used to refer to the above systems as either "LILO"[4] or "GRUB" systems.

Unfortunately, nobody ever understood what I was talking about; now I just use the word "GNU" as a pseudonym for GRUB.

So, if you ever hear people talking about their alleged "GNU" systems, remember that they are actually paying homage to the best boot loader around... GRUB!

We, the GRUB maintainers, do not (usually) encourage Gordon's level of fanaticism, but it helps to remember that boot loaders deserve recognition. We hope that you enjoy using GNU GRUB as much as we did writing it.

---

[4] The LInux LOader, a boot loader that everybody uses, but nobody likes.

2 Naming convention

The device syntax used in GRUB is a wee bit different from what you may have seen before in your operating system(s), and you need to know it so that you can specify a drive/partition.

Look at the following examples and explanations:

`(fd0)`

First of all, GRUB requires that the device name be enclosed with '(' and ')'. The 'fd' part means that it is a floppy disk. The number '0' is the drive number, which is counted from *zero*. This expression means that GRUB will use the whole floppy disk.

`(hd0,msdos2)`

Here, 'hd' means it is a hard disk drive. The first integer '0' indicates the drive number, that is, the first hard disk, the string 'msdos' indicates the partition scheme, while the second integer, '2', indicates the partition number (or the PC slice number in the BSD terminology). The partition numbers are counted from *one*, not from zero (as was the case in previous versions of GRUB). This expression means the second partition of the first hard disk drive. In this case, GRUB uses one partition of the disk, instead of the whole disk.

`(hd0,msdos5)`

This specifies the first *extended partition* of the first hard disk drive. Note that the partition numbers for extended partitions are counted from '5', regardless of the actual number of primary partitions on your hard disk.

`(hd1,msdos1,bsd1)`

This means the BSD 'a' partition on first PC slice number of the second hard disk.

Of course, to actually access the disks or partitions with GRUB, you need to use the device specification in a command, like 'set root=(fd0)' or 'parttool (hd0,msdos3) hidden-'. To help you find out which number specifies a partition you want, the GRUB command-line (see Section 12.1 [Command-line interface], page 45) options have argument completion. This means that, for example, you only need to type

`set root=(`

followed by a TAB, and GRUB will display the list of drives, partitions, or file names. So it should be quite easy to determine the name of your target partition, even with minimal knowledge of the syntax.

Note that GRUB does *not* distinguish IDE from SCSI - it simply counts the drive numbers from zero, regardless of their type. Normally, any IDE drive number is less than any SCSI drive number, although that is not true if you change the boot sequence by swapping IDE and SCSI drives in your BIOS.

Now the question is, how to specify a file? Again, consider an example:

`(hd0,msdos1)/vmlinuz`

This specifies the file named 'vmlinuz', found on the first partition of the first hard disk drive. Note that the argument completion works with file names, too.

That was easy, admit it. Now read the next chapter, to find out how to actually install GRUB on your drive.

3 Installation

In order to install GRUB as your boot loader, you need to first install the GRUB system and utilities under your UNIX-like operating system (see Appendix A [Obtaining and Building GRUB], page 107). You can do this either from the source tarball, or as a package for your OS.

After you have done that, you need to install the boot loader on a drive (floppy or hard disk) by using the utility **grub-install** (see Chapter 28 [Invoking grub-install], page 97) on a UNIX-like OS.

GRUB comes with boot images, which are normally put in the directory '/usr/lib/grub/<cpu>-<platform>' (for BIOS-based machines '/usr/lib/grub/i386-pc'). Hereafter, the directory where GRUB images are initially placed (normally '/usr/lib/grub/<cpu>-<platform>') will be called the *image directory*, and the directory where the boot loader needs to find them (usually '/boot') will be called the *boot directory*.

3.1 Installing GRUB using grub-install

For information on where GRUB should be installed on PC BIOS platforms, see Section 3.4 [BIOS installation], page 11.

In order to install GRUB under a UNIX-like OS (such as GNU), invoke the program **grub-install** (see Chapter 28 [Invoking grub-install], page 97) as the superuser (*root*).

The usage is basically very simple. You only need to specify one argument to the program, namely, where to install the boot loader. The argument has to be either a device file (like '/dev/hda'). For example, under Linux the following will install GRUB into the MBR of the first IDE disk:

```
# grub-install /dev/hda
```

Likewise, under GNU/Hurd, this has the same effect:

```
# grub-install /dev/hd0
```

But all the above examples assume that GRUB should put images under the '/boot' directory. If you want GRUB to put images under a directory other than '/boot', you need to specify the option '--boot-directory'. The typical usage is that you create a GRUB boot floppy with a filesystem. Here is an example:

```
# mke2fs /dev/fd0
# mount -t ext2 /dev/fd0 /mnt
# mkdir /mnt/boot
# grub-install --boot-directory=/mnt/boot /dev/fd0
# umount /mnt
```

Some BIOSes have a bug of exposing the first partition of a USB drive as a floppy instead of exposing the USB drive as a hard disk (they call it "USB-FDD" boot). In such cases, you need to install like this:

```
# losetup /dev/loop0 /dev/sdb1
# mount /dev/loop0 /mnt/usb
# grub-install --boot-directory=/mnt/usb/bugbios --force --allow-floppy /d
```

This install doesn't conflict with standard install as long as they are in separate directories.

Note that `grub-install` is actually just a shell script and the real task is done by `grub-mkimage` and `grub-setup`. Therefore, you may run those commands directly to install GRUB, without using `grub-install`. Don't do that, however, unless you are very familiar with the internals of GRUB. Installing a boot loader on a running OS may be extremely dangerous.

3.2 Making a GRUB bootable CD-ROM

GRUB supports the *no emulation mode* in the El Torito specification[1]. This means that you can use the whole CD-ROM from GRUB and you don't have to make a floppy or hard disk image file, which can cause compatibility problems.

For booting from a CD-ROM, GRUB uses a special image called 'cdboot.img', which is concatenated with 'core.img'. The 'core.img' used for this should be built with at least the 'iso9660' and 'biosdisk' modules. Your bootable CD-ROM will usually also need to include a configuration file 'grub.cfg' and some other GRUB modules.

To make a simple generic GRUB rescue CD, you can use the `grub-mkrescue` program (see Chapter 31 [Invoking grub-mkrescue], page 103):

```
$ grub-mkrescue -o grub.iso
```

You will often need to include other files in your image. To do this, first make a top directory for the bootable image, say, 'iso':

```
$ mkdir iso
```

Make a directory for GRUB:

```
$ mkdir -p iso/boot/grub
```

If desired, make the config file 'grub.cfg' under 'iso/boot/grub' (see Chapter 5 [Configuration], page 17), and copy any files and directories for the disc to the directory 'iso/'.

Finally, make the image:

```
$ grub-mkrescue -o grub.iso iso
```

This produces a file named 'grub.iso', which then can be burned into a CD (or a DVD), or written to a USB mass storage device.

The root device will be set up appropriately on entering your 'grub.cfg' configuration file, so you can refer to file names on the CD without needing to use an explicit device name. This makes it easier to produce rescue images that will work on both optical drives and USB mass storage devices.

3.3 The map between BIOS drives and OS devices

If the device map file exists, the GRUB utilities (`grub-probe`, `grub-setup`, etc.) read it to map BIOS drives to OS devices. This file consists of lines like this:

---

[1] El Torito is a specification for bootable CD using BIOS functions.

`(device) file`

device is a drive specified in the GRUB syntax (see Section 11.1 [Device syntax], page 43), and *file* is an OS file, which is normally a device file.

Historically, the device map file was used because GRUB device names had to be used in the configuration file, and they were derived from BIOS drive numbers. The map between BIOS drives and OS devices cannot always be guessed correctly: for example, GRUB will get the order wrong if you exchange the boot sequence between IDE and SCSI in your BIOS.

Unfortunately, even OS device names are not always stable. Modern versions of the Linux kernel may probe drives in a different order from boot to boot, and the prefix (`/dev/hd*` versus `/dev/sd*`) may change depending on the driver subsystem in use. As a result, the device map file required frequent editing on some systems.

GRUB avoids this problem nowadays by using UUIDs or file system labels when generating '`grub.cfg`', and we advise that you do the same for any custom menu entries you write. If the device map file does not exist, then the GRUB utilities will assume a temporary device map on the fly. This is often good enough, particularly in the common case of single-disk systems.

However, the device map file is not entirely obsolete yet, and it is used for overriding when current environment is different from the one on boot. Most common case is if you use a partition or logical volume as a disk for virtual machine. You can put any comments in the file if needed, as the GRUB utilities assume that a line is just a comment if the first character is '`#`'.

3.4 BIOS installation

MBR

The partition table format traditionally used on PC BIOS platforms is called the Master Boot Record (MBR) format; this is the format that allows up to four primary partitions and additional logical partitions. With this partition table format, there are two ways to install GRUB: it can be embedded in the area between the MBR and the first partition (called by various names, such as the "boot track", "MBR gap", or "embedding area", and which is usually at least 31 KiB), or the core image can be installed in a file system and a list of the blocks that make it up can be stored in the first sector of that partition.

Each of these has different problems. There is no way to reserve space in the embedding area with complete safety, and some proprietary software is known to use it to make it difficult for users to work around licensing restrictions; and systems are sometimes partitioned without leaving enough space before the first partition. On the other hand, installing to a filesystem means that GRUB is vulnerable to its blocks being moved around by filesystem features such as tail packing, or even by aggressive fsck implementations, so this approach is quite fragile; and this approach can only be used if the '`/boot`' filesystem is on the same disk that the BIOS boots from, so that GRUB does not have to rely on guessing BIOS drive numbers.

The GRUB development team generally recommends embedding GRUB before the first partition, unless you have special requirements. You must ensure that the first partition starts at least 31 KiB (63 sectors) from the start of the disk; on modern disks, it is often a performance advantage to align partitions on larger boundaries anyway, so the first partition might start 1 MiB from the start of the disk.

GPT

Some newer systems use the GUID Partition Table (GPT) format. This was specified as part of the Extensible Firmware Interface (EFI), but it can also be used on BIOS platforms if system software supports it; for example, GRUB and GNU/Linux can be used in this configuration. With this format, it is possible to reserve a whole partition for GRUB, called the BIOS Boot Partition. GRUB can then be embedded into that partition without the risk of being overwritten by other software and without being contained in a filesystem which might move its blocks around.

When creating a BIOS Boot Partition on a GPT system, you should make sure that it is at least 31 KiB in size. (GPT-formatted disks are not usually particularly small, so we recommend that you make it larger than the bare minimum, such as 1 MiB, to allow plenty of room for growth.) You must also make sure that it has the proper partition type. Using GNU Parted, you can set this using a command such as the following:

```
# parted /dev/disk set partition-number bios_grub on
```

If you are using gdisk, set the partition type to 'OxEF02'. With partitioning programs that require setting the GUID directly, it should be '21686148-6449-6e6f-744e656564454649'.

Caution: Be very careful which partition you select! When GRUB finds a BIOS Boot Partition during installation, it will automatically overwrite part of it. Make sure that the partition does not contain any other data.

4 Booting

GRUB can load Multiboot-compliant kernels in a consistent way, but for some free operating systems you need to use some OS-specific magic.

4.1 How to boot operating systems

GRUB has two distinct boot methods. One of the two is to load an operating system directly, and the other is to chain-load another boot loader which then will load an operating system actually. Generally speaking, the former is more desirable, because you don't need to install or maintain other boot loaders and GRUB is flexible enough to load an operating system from an arbitrary disk/partition. However, the latter is sometimes required, since GRUB doesn't support all the existing operating systems natively.

4.1.1 How to boot an OS directly with GRUB

Multiboot (see Section "Motivation" in *The Multiboot Specification*) is the native format supported by GRUB. For the sake of convenience, there is also support for Linux, FreeBSD, NetBSD and OpenBSD. If you want to boot other operating systems, you will have to chain-load them (see Section 4.1.2 [Chain-loading], page 13).

FIXME: this section is incomplete.

1. Run the command `boot` (see Section 14.3.4 [boot], page 56).

However, DOS and Windows have some deficiencies, so you might have to use more complicated instructions. See Section 4.3.3 [DOS/Windows], page 15, for more information.

4.1.2 Chain-loading an OS

Operating systems that do not support Multiboot and do not have specific support in GRUB (specific support is available for Linux, FreeBSD, NetBSD and OpenBSD) must be chain-loaded, which involves loading another boot loader and jumping to it in real mode.

The `chainloader` command (see Section 14.3.6 [chainloader], page 56) is used to set this up. It is normally also necessary to load some GRUB modules and set the appropriate root device. Putting this together, we get something like this, for a Windows system on the first partition of the first hard disk:

```
menuentry "Windows" {
        insmod chain
        insmod ntfs
        set root=(hd0,1)
        chainloader +1
}
```

On systems with multiple hard disks, an additional workaround may be required. See Section 4.3.3 [DOS/Windows], page 15.

Chain-loading is only supported on PC BIOS and EFI platforms.

4.2 Loopback booting

GRUB is able to read from an image (be it one of CD or HDD) stored on any of its accessible storages (refer to see Section 14.3.28 [loopback], page 60 command). However the OS itself should be able to find its root. This usually involves running a userspace program running before the real root is discovered. This is achieved by GRUB loading a specially made small image and passing it as ramdisk to the kernel. This is achieved by commands `kfreebsd_module`, `knetbsd_module_elf`, `kopenbsd_ramdisk`, `initrd` (see Section 14.3.20 [initrd], page 59), `initrd16` (see Section 14.3.20 [initrd], page 59), `multiboot_module`, `multiboot2_module` or `xnu_ramdisk` depending on the loader. Note that for knetbsd the image must be put inside miniroot.kmod and the whole miniroot.kmod has to be loaded. In kopenbsd payload this is disabled by default. Aditionally behaviour of initial ramdisk depends on command line options. Several distributors provide the image for this purpose or it's integrated in their standard ramdisk and activated by special option. Consult your kernel and distribution manual for more details. Other loaders like appleloader, chainloader (BIOS, EFI, coreboot), freedos, ntldr and plan9 provide no possibility of loading initial ramdisk and as far as author is aware the payloads in question don't support either initial ramdisk or discovering loopback boot in other way and as such not bootable this way. Please consider alternative boot methods like copying all files from the image to actual partition. Consult your OS documentation for more details

4.3 Some caveats on OS-specific issues

Here, we describe some caveats on several operating systems.

4.3.1 GNU/Hurd

Since GNU/Hurd is Multiboot-compliant, it is easy to boot it; there is nothing special about it. But do not forget that you have to specify a root partition to the kernel.

1. Set GRUB's root device to the same drive as GNU/Hurd's. The command `search --set=root --file /boot/gnumach.gz` or similar may help you (see Section 14.3.40 [search], page 63).

2. Load the kernel and the modules, like this:

```
grub> multiboot /boot/gnumach.gz root=device:hd0s1
grub> module  /hurd/ext2fs.static ext2fs --readonly \
                  --multiboot-command-line='${kernel-command-line}' \
                  --host-priv-port='${host-port}' \
                  --device-master-port='${device-port}' \
                  --exec-server-task='${exec-task}' -T typed '${root}'
                  '$(task-create)' '$(task-resume)'
grub> module /lib/ld.so.1 exec /hurd/exec '$(exec-task=task-create)'
```

3. Finally, run the command `boot` (see Section 14.3.4 [boot], page 56).

4.3.2 GNU/Linux

It is relatively easy to boot GNU/Linux from GRUB, because it somewhat resembles to boot a Multiboot-compliant OS.

1. Set GRUB's root device to the same drive as GNU/Linux's. The command **search** `--set=root --file /vmlinuz` or similar may help you (see Section 14.3.40 [search], page 63).

2. Load the kernel using the command **linux** (see Section 14.3.24 [linux], page 60):

   grub> *linux /vmlinuz root=/dev/sda1*

   If you need to specify some kernel parameters, just append them to the command. For example, to set 'acpi' to 'off', do this:

   grub> *linux /vmlinuz root=/dev/sda1 acpi=off*

   See the documentation in the Linux source tree for complete information on the available options.

   With **linux** GRUB uses 32-bit protocol. Some BIOS services like APM or EDD aren't available with this protocol. In this case you need to use **linux16**

   grub> *linux16 /vmlinuz root=/dev/sda1 acpi=off*

3. If you use an initrd, execute the command **initrd** (see Section 14.3.20 [initrd], page 59) after **linux**:

   grub> *initrd /initrd*

   If you used **linux16** you need to use **initrd16**:

   grub> *initrd16 /initrd*

4. Finally, run the command **boot** (see Section 14.3.4 [boot], page 56).

Caution: If you use an initrd and specify the 'mem=' option to the kernel to let it use less than actual memory size, you will also have to specify the same memory size to GRUB. To let GRUB know the size, run the command **uppermem** *before* loading the kernel. See Section 14.3.45 [uppermem], page 66, for more information.

4.3.3 DOS/Windows

GRUB cannot boot DOS or Windows directly, so you must chain-load them (see Section 4.1.2 [Chain-loading], page 13). However, their boot loaders have some critical deficiencies, so it may not work to just chain-load them. To overcome the problems, GRUB provides you with two helper functions.

If you have installed DOS (or Windows) on a non-first hard disk, you have to use the disk swapping technique, because that OS cannot boot from any disks but the first one. The workaround used in GRUB is the command **drivemap** (see Section 14.3.12 [drivemap], page 57), like this:

drivemap -s (hd0) (hd1)

This performs a *virtual* swap between your first and second hard drive.

Caution: This is effective only if DOS (or Windows) uses BIOS to access the swapped disks. If that OS uses a special driver for the disks, this probably won't work.

Another problem arises if you installed more than one set of DOS/Windows onto one disk, because they could be confused if there are more than one primary partitions for DOS/Windows. Certainly you should avoid doing this, but there is a solution if you do want to do so. Use the partition hiding/unhiding technique.

If GRUB *hides* a DOS (or Windows) partition (see Section 14.3.32 [parttool], page 61), DOS (or Windows) will ignore the partition. If GRUB *unhides* a DOS (or

Windows) partition, DOS (or Windows) will detect the partition. Thus, if you have installed DOS (or Windows) on the first and the second partition of the first hard disk, and you want to boot the copy on the first partition, do the following:

```
parttool (hd0,1) hidden-
parttool (hd0,2) hidden+
set root=(hd0,1)
chainloader +1
parttool ${root} boot+
boot
```

5 Writing your own configuration file

GRUB is configured using 'grub.cfg', usually located under '/boot/grub'. This file is quite flexible, but most users will not need to write the whole thing by hand.

5.1 Simple configuration handling

The program grub-mkconfig (see Chapter 29 [Invoking grub-mkconfig], page 99) generates 'grub.cfg' files suitable for most cases. It is suitable for use when upgrading a distribution, and will discover available kernels and attempt to generate menu entries for them.

grub-mkconfig does have some limitations. While adding extra custom menu entries to the end of the list can be done by editing '/etc/grub.d/40_custom' or creating '/boot/grub/custom.cfg', changing the order of menu entries or changing their titles may require making complex changes to shell scripts stored in '/etc/grub.d/'. This may be improved in the future. In the meantime, those who feel that it would be easier to write 'grub.cfg' directly are encouraged to do so (see Chapter 4 [Booting], page 13, and Section 5.2 [Shell-like scripting], page 21), and to disable any system provided by their distribution to automatically run grub-mkconfig.

The file '/etc/default/grub' controls the operation of grub-mkconfig. It is sourced by a shell script, and so must be valid POSIX shell input; normally, it will just be a sequence of 'KEY=value' lines, but if the value contains spaces or other special characters then it must be quoted. For example:

```
GRUB_TERMINAL_INPUT="console serial"
```

Valid keys in '/etc/default/grub' are as follows:

'GRUB_DEFAULT'

> The default menu entry. This may be a number, in which case it identifies the Nth entry in the generated menu counted from zero, or the title of a menu entry, or the special string 'saved'. Using the title may be useful if you want to set a menu entry as the default even though there may be a variable number of entries before it.
>
> For example, if you have:
>
> ```
> menuentry 'Example GNU/Linux distribution' --class gnu-linux {
>         ...
> }
> ```
>
> then you can make this the default using:
>
> ```
> GRUB_DEFAULT='Example GNU/Linux distribution'
> ```
>
> If you set this to 'saved', then the default menu entry will be that saved by 'GRUB_SAVEDEFAULT', grub-set-default, or grub-reboot.
>
> The default is '0'.

'GRUB_SAVEDEFAULT'

> If this option is set to 'true', then, when an entry is selected, save it as a new default entry for use by future runs of GRUB. This is only useful if 'GRUB_DEFAULT=saved'; it is a separate option because 'GRUB_DEFAULT=saved'

is useful without this option, in conjunction with `grub-set-default` or `grub-reboot`. Unset by default. This option relies on the environment block, which may not be available in all situations (see Section 13.2 [Environment block], page 51).

'GRUB_TIMEOUT'

Boot the default entry this many seconds after the menu is displayed, unless a key is pressed. The default is '5'. Set to '0' to boot immediately without displaying the menu, or to '-1' to wait indefinitely.

'GRUB_HIDDEN_TIMEOUT'

Wait this many seconds for a key to be pressed before displaying the menu. If no key is pressed during that time, display the menu for the number of seconds specified in GRUB_TIMEOUT before booting the default entry. We expect that most people who use GRUB_HIDDEN_TIMEOUT will want to have GRUB_TIMEOUT set to '0' so that the menu is not displayed at all unless a key is pressed. Unset by default.

'GRUB_HIDDEN_TIMEOUT_QUIET'

In conjunction with 'GRUB_HIDDEN_TIMEOUT', set this to 'true' to suppress the verbose countdown while waiting for a key to be pressed before displaying the menu. Unset by default.

'GRUB_DEFAULT_BUTTON'
'GRUB_TIMEOUT_BUTTON'
'GRUB_HIDDEN_TIMEOUT_BUTTON'
'GRUB_BUTTON_CMOS_ADDRESS'

Variants of the corresponding variables without the '_BUTTON' suffix, used to support vendor-specific power buttons. See Chapter 9 [Vendor power-on keys], page 39.

'GRUB_DISTRIBUTOR'

Set by distributors of GRUB to their identifying name. This is used to generate more informative menu entry titles.

'GRUB_TERMINAL_INPUT'

Select the terminal input device. You may select multiple devices here, separated by spaces.

Valid terminal input names depend on the platform, but may include 'console' (PC BIOS and EFI consoles), 'serial' (serial terminal), 'ofconsole' (Open Firmware console), 'at_keyboard' (PC AT keyboard, mainly useful with Coreboot), or 'usb_keyboard' (USB keyboard using the HID Boot Protocol, for cases where the firmware does not handle this).

The default is to use the platform's native terminal input.

'GRUB_TERMINAL_OUTPUT'

Select the terminal output device. You may select multiple devices here, separated by spaces.

Valid terminal output names depend on the platform, but may include 'console' (PC BIOS and EFI consoles), 'serial' (serial terminal), 'gfxterm' (graphics-mode output), 'ofconsole' (Open Firmware console), or 'vga_text' (VGA text output, mainly useful with Coreboot).

The default is to use the platform's native terminal output.

'GRUB_TERMINAL'

If this option is set, it overrides both 'GRUB_TERMINAL_INPUT' and 'GRUB_TERMINAL_OUTPUT' to the same value.

'GRUB_SERIAL_COMMAND'

A command to configure the serial port when using the serial console. See Section 14.2.1 [serial], page 54. Defaults to 'serial'.

'GRUB_CMDLINE_LINUX'

Command-line arguments to add to menu entries for the Linux kernel.

'GRUB_CMDLINE_LINUX_DEFAULT'

Unless 'GRUB_DISABLE_RECOVERY' is set to 'true', two menu entries will be generated for each Linux kernel: one default entry and one entry for recovery mode. This option lists command-line arguments to add only to the default menu entry, after those listed in 'GRUB_CMDLINE_LINUX'.

'GRUB_CMDLINE_NETBSD'
'GRUB_CMDLINE_NETBSD_DEFAULT'

As 'GRUB_CMDLINE_LINUX' and 'GRUB_CMDLINE_LINUX_DEFAULT', but for NetBSD.

'GRUB_CMDLINE_GNUMACH'

As 'GRUB_CMDLINE_LINUX', but for GNU Mach.

'GRUB_CMDLINE_XEN'
'GRUB_CMDLINE_XEN_DEFAULT'

The values of these options are appended to the values of 'GRUB_CMDLINE_LINUX' and 'GRUB_CMDLINE_LINUX_DEFAULT' for Linux and Xen menu entries.

'GRUB_CMDLINE_LINUX_XEN_REPLACE'
'GRUB_CMDLINE_LINUX_XEN_REPLACE_DEFAULT'

The values of these options replace the values of 'GRUB_CMDLINE_LINUX' and 'GRUB_CMDLINE_LINUX_DEFAULT' for Linux and Xen menu entries.

'GRUB_DISABLE_LINUX_UUID'

Normally, grub-mkconfig will generate menu entries that use universally-unique identifiers (UUIDs) to identify the root filesystem to the Linux kernel, using a 'root=UUID=...' kernel parameter. This is usually more reliable, but in some cases it may not be appropriate. To disable the use of UUIDs, set this option to 'true'.

'GRUB_DISABLE_RECOVERY'

If this option is set to 'true', disable the generation of recovery mode menu entries.

'GRUB_VIDEO_BACKEND'

If graphical video support is required, either because the 'gfxterm' graphical terminal is in use or because 'GRUB_GFXPAYLOAD_LINUX' is set, then grub-mkconfig will normally load all available GRUB video drivers and use the one most appropriate for your hardware. If you need to override this for some reason, then you can set this option.

After `grub-install` has been run, the available video drivers are listed in '`/boot/grub/video.lst`'.

'GRUB_GFXMODE'

Set the resolution used on the '`gfxterm`' graphical terminal. Note that you can only use modes which your graphics card supports via VESA BIOS Extensions (VBE), so for example native LCD panel resolutions may not be available. The default is '`auto`', which tries to select a preferred resolution. See Section 13.1.8 [gfxmode], page 49.

'GRUB_BACKGROUND'

Set a background image for use with the '`gfxterm`' graphical terminal. The value of this option must be a file readable by GRUB at boot time, and it must end with '`.png`', '`.tga`', '`.jpg`', or '`.jpeg`'. The image will be scaled if necessary to fit the screen.

'GRUB_THEME'

Set a theme for use with the '`gfxterm`' graphical terminal.

'GRUB_GFXPAYLOAD_LINUX'

Set to '`text`' to force the Linux kernel to boot in normal text mode, '`keep`' to preserve the graphics mode set using '`GRUB_GFXMODE`', '`widthxheight`'['`xdepth`'] to set a particular graphics mode, or a sequence of these separated by commas or semicolons to try several modes in sequence. See Section 13.1.9 [gfxpayload], page 49.

Depending on your kernel, your distribution, your graphics card, and the phase of the moon, note that using this option may cause GNU/Linux to suffer from various display problems, particularly during the early part of the boot sequence. If you have problems, set this option to '`text`' and GRUB will tell Linux to boot in normal text mode.

'GRUB_DISABLE_OS_PROBER'

Normally, `grub-mkconfig` will try to use the external `os-prober` program, if installed, to discover other operating systems installed on the same system and generate appropriate menu entries for them. Set this option to '`true`' to disable this.

'GRUB_INIT_TUNE'

Play a tune on the speaker when GRUB starts. This is particularly useful for users unable to see the screen. The value of this option is passed directly to Section 14.3.35 [play], page 62.

'GRUB_BADRAM'

If this option is set, GRUB will issue a Section 14.3.2 [badram], page 55 command to filter out specified regions of RAM.

'GRUB_PRELOAD_MODULES'

This option may be set to a list of GRUB module names separated by spaces. Each module will be loaded as early as possible, at the start of '`grub.cfg`'.

For more detailed customisation of `grub-mkconfig`'s output, you may edit the scripts in '/etc/grub.d' directly. '/etc/grub.d/40_custom' is particularly useful for adding entire custom menu entries; simply type the menu entries you want to add at the end of that file, making sure to leave at least the first two lines intact.

5.2 Writing full configuration files directly

'grub.cfg' is written in GRUB's built-in scripting language, which has a syntax quite similar to that of GNU Bash and other Bourne shell derivatives.

Words

A *word* is a sequence of characters considered as a single unit by GRUB. Words are separated by *metacharacters*, which are the following plus space, tab, and newline:

```
{ } | & $ ; < >
```

Quoting may be used to include metacharacters in words; see below.

Reserved words

Reserved words have a special meaning to GRUB. The following words are recognised as reserved when unquoted and either the first word of a simple command or the third word of a `for` command:

```
! [[ ]] { }
case do done elif else esac fi for function
if in menuentry select then time until while
```

Not all of these reserved words have a useful purpose yet; some are reserved for future expansion.

Quoting

Quoting is used to remove the special meaning of certain characters or words. It can be used to treat metacharacters as part of a word, to prevent reserved words from being recognised as such, and to prevent variable expansion.

There are three quoting mechanisms: the escape character, single quotes, and double quotes.

A non-quoted backslash (\) is the *escape character*. It preserves the literal value of the next character that follows, with the exception of newline.

Enclosing characters in single quotes preserves the literal value of each character within the quotes. A single quote may not occur between single quotes, even when preceded by a backslash.

Enclosing characters in double quotes preserves the literal value of all characters within the quotes, with the exception of '$' and '\'. The '$' character retains its special meaning within double quotes. The backslash retains its special meaning only when followed by one of the following characters: '$', '"', '\', or newline. A backslash-newline pair is treated as a line continuation (that is, it is removed from the input stream and effectively ignored[1]). A double quote may be quoted within double quotes by preceding it with a backslash.

Variable expansion

The '$' character introduces variable expansion. The variable name to be expanded may be enclosed in braces, which are optional but serve to protect the variable to be expanded from characters immediately following it which could be interpreted as part of the name.

Normal variable names begin with an alphabetic character, followed by zero or more alphanumeric characters. These names refer to entries in the GRUB environment (see Chapter 13 [Environment], page 47).

Positional variable names consist of one or more digits. They represent parameters passed to function calls, with '$1' representing the first parameter, and so on.

The special variable name '?' expands to the exit status of the most recently executed command. When positional variable names are active, other special variable names '@', '*' and '#' are defined and they expand to all positional parameters with necessary quoting, positional parameters without any quoting, and positional parameter count respectively.

Comments

A word beginning with '#' causes that word and all remaining characters on that line to be ignored.

Simple commands

A *simple command* is a sequence of words separated by spaces or tabs and terminated by a semicolon or a newline. The first word specifies the command to be executed. The remaining words are passed as arguments to the invoked command.

The return value of a simple command is its exit status. If the reserved word ! precedes the command, then the return value is instead the logical negation of the command's exit status.

Compound commands

A *compound command* is one of the following:

for *name* in *word* . . .; do *list*; done

> The list of words following **in** is expanded, generating a list of items. The variable *name* is set to each element of this list in turn, and *list* is executed each time. The return value is the exit status of the last command that executes. If the expansion of the items following **in** results in an empty list, no commands are executed, and the return status is 0.

if *list*; then *list*; [elif *list*; then *list*;] . . . [else *list*;] fi

> The **if** *list* is executed. If its exit status is zero, the **then** *list* is executed. Otherwise, each **elif** *list* is executed in turn, and if its exit status is zero, the

---

[1] Currently a backslash-newline pair within a variable name is not handled properly, so use this feature with some care.

corresponding **then** *list* is executed and the command completes. Otherwise, the **else** *list* is executed, if present. The exit status is the exit status of the last command executed, or zero if no condition tested true.

while *cond*; do *list*; done
until *cond*; do *list*; done

> The **while** command continuously executes the **do** *list* as long as the last command in *cond* returns an exit status of zero. The **until** command is identical to the **while** command, except that the test is negated; the **do** *list* is executed as long as the last command in *cond* returns a non-zero exit status. The exit status of the **while** and **until** commands is the exit status of the last **do** *list* command executed, or zero if none was executed.

function *name* { *command*; ... }

> This defines a function named *name*. The *body* of the function is the list of commands within braces, each of which must be terminated with a semicolon or a newline. This list of commands will be executed whenever *name* is specified as the name of a simple command. Function definitions do not affect the exit status in **$?**. When executed, the exit status of a function is the exit status of the last command executed in the body.

menuentry *title* ['--class=class' ...] ['--users=users'] ['--unrestricted']
['--hotkey=key'] { *command*; ... }

> See Section 14.1.1 [menuentry], page 53.

Built-in Commands

Some built-in commands are also provided by GRUB script to help script writers perform actions that are otherwise not possible. For example, these include commands to jump out of a loop without fully completing it, etc.

break [n]
> Exit from within a **for**, **while**, or **until** loop. If n is specified, break n levels. n must be greater than or equal to 1. If n is greater than the number of enclosing loops, all enclosing loops are exited. The return value is 0 unless n is not greater than or equal to 1.

continue [n]
> Resume the next iteration of the enclosing **for**, **while** or **until** loop. If n is specified, resume at the nth enclosing loop. n must be greater than or equal to 1. If n is greater than the number of enclosing loops, the last enclosing loop (the *top-level* loop) is resumed. The return value is 0 unless n is not greater than or equal to 1.

return [n]
> Causes a function to exit with the return value specified by n. If n is omitted, the return status is that of the last command executed in the function body. If used outside a function the return status is false.

shift [n]
> The positional parameters from n+1 ... are renamed to $1.... Parameters represented by the numbers $# down to $#-n+1 are unset. n must be a non-negative number less than or equal to $#. If n is 0, no parameters are changed. If n is not given, it is assumed to be 1. If n is greater than $#, the positional

parameters are not changed. The return status is greater than zero if `n` is greater than `$#` or less than zero; otherwise 0.

5.3 Multi-boot manual config

Currently autogenerating config files for multi-boot environments depends on os-prober and has several shortcomings. While fixing it is scheduled for the next release, meanwhile you can make use of the power of GRUB syntax and do it yourself. A possible configuration is detailed here, feel free to adjust to your needs.

First create a separate GRUB partition, big enough to hold GRUB. Some of the following entries show how to load OS installer images from this same partition, for that you obviously need to make the partition large enough to hold those images as well. Mount this partition on/mnt/boot and disable GRUB in all OSes and manually install self-compiled latest GRUB with:

```
grub-install --boot-directory=/mnt/boot /dev/sda
```

In all the OSes install GRUB tools but disable installing GRUB in bootsector, so you'll have menu.lst and grub.cfg available for use. Also disable os-prober use by setting:

```
GRUB_DISABLE_OS_PROBER=true
```

in /etc/default/grub

Then write a grub.cfg (/mnt/boot/grub/grub.cfg):

```
menuentry "OS using grub2" {
    insmod xfs
    search --set=root --label OS1 --hint hd0,msdos8
    configfile /boot/grub/grub.cfg
}

menuentry "OS using grub2-legacy" {
    insmod ext2
    search --set=root --label OS2 --hint hd0,msdos6
    legacy_configfile /boot/grub/menu.lst
}

menuentry "Windows XP" {
    insmod ntfs
    search --set=root --label WINDOWS_XP --hint hd0,msdos1
    ntldr /ntldr
}

menuentry "Windows 7" {
    insmod ntfs
    search --set=root --label WINDOWS_7 --hint hd0,msdos2
    ntldr /bootmgr
}

menuentry "FreeBSD" {
```

```
        insmod zfs
        search --set=root --label freepool --hint hd0,msdos7
        kfreebsd /freebsd@/boot/kernel/kernel
        kfreebsd_module_elf /freebsd@/boot/kernel/opensolaris.ko
        kfreebsd_module_elf /freebsd@/boot/kernel/zfs.ko
        kfreebsd_module /freebsd@/boot/zfs/zpool.cache type=/boot/zfs/zp(
        set kFreeBSD.vfs.root.mountfrom=zfs:freepool/freebsd
        set kFreeBSD.hw.psm.synaptics_support=1
}

menuentry "experimental GRUB" {
        search --set=root --label GRUB --hint hd0,msdos5
        multiboot /experimental/grub/i386-pc/core.img
}

menuentry "Fedora 16 installer" {
        search --set=root --label GRUB --hint hd0,msdos5
        linux /fedora/vmlinuz lang=en_US keymap=sg resolution=1280x800
        initrd /fedora/initrd.img
}

menuentry "Fedora rawhide installer" {
        search --set=root --label GRUB --hint hd0,msdos5
        linux /fedora/vmlinuz repo=ftp://mirror.switch.ch/mirror/fedora/:
        initrd /fedora/initrd.img
}

menuentry "Debian sid installer" {
        search --set=root --label GRUB --hint hd0,msdos5
        linux /debian/dists/sid/main/installer-amd64/current/images/hd-m(
        initrd /debian/dists/sid/main/installer-amd64/current/images/hd-r
}
```

Notes:

- Argument to search after –label is FS LABEL. You can also use UUIDs with –fs-uuid UUID instead of –label LABEL. You could also use direct `root=hd0,msdosX` but this is not recommened due to device name instability.

5.4 Embedding a configuration file into GRUB

GRUB supports embedding a configuration file directly into the core image, so that it is loaded before entering normal mode. This is useful, for example, when it is not straightforward to find the real configuration file, or when you need to debug problems with loading that file. `grub-install` uses this feature when it is not using BIOS disk functions or when installing to a different disk from the one containing '/boot/grub', in which case it needs to use the `search` command (see Section 14.3.40 [search], page 63) to find '/boot/grub'.

To embed a configuration file, use the '-c' option to grub-mkimage. The file is copied into the core image, so it may reside anywhere on the file system, and may be removed after running grub-mkimage.

After the embedded configuration file (if any) is executed, GRUB will load the 'normal' module (see Section 14.3.30 [normal], page 61), which will then read the real configuration file from '$prefix/grub.cfg'. By this point, the root variable will also have been set to the root device name. For example, prefix might be set to '(hd0,1)/boot/grub', and root might be set to 'hd0,1'. Thus, in most cases, the embedded configuration file only needs to set the prefix and root variables, and then drop through to GRUB's normal processing. A typical example of this might look like this:

```
search.fs_uuid 01234567-89ab-cdef-0123-456789abcdef root
set prefix=($root)/boot/grub
```

(The 'search_fs_uuid' module must be included in the core image for this example to work.)

In more complex cases, it may be useful to read other configuration files directly from the embedded configuration file. This allows such things as reading files not called 'grub.cfg', or reading files from a directory other than that where GRUB's loadable modules are installed. To do this, include the 'configfile' and 'normal' modules in the core image, and embed a configuration file that uses the configfile command to load another file. The following example of this also requires the echo, search_label, and test modules to be included in the core image:

```
search.fs_label grub root
if [ -e /boot/grub/example/test1.cfg ]; then
    set prefix=($root)/boot/grub
    configfile /boot/grub/example/test1.cfg
else
    if [ -e /boot/grub/example/test2.cfg ]; then
        set prefix=($root)/boot/grub
        configfile /boot/grub/example/test2.cfg
    else
        echo "Could not find an example configuration file!"
    fi
fi
```

The embedded configuration file may not contain menu entries directly, but may only read them from elsewhere using configfile.

6 Theme file format

6.1 Introduction

The GRUB graphical menu supports themes that can customize the layout and appearance of the GRUB boot menu. The theme is configured through a plain text file that specifies the layout of the various GUI components (including the boot menu, timeout progress bar, and text messages) as well as the appearance using colors, fonts, and images. Example is available in docs/example_theme.txt

6.2 Theme Elements

6.2.1 Colors

Colors can be specified in several ways:

- HTML-style "#RRGGBB" or "#RGB" format, where *R*, *G*, and *B* are hexadecimal digits (e.g., "#8899FF")
- as comma-separated decimal RGB values (e.g., "128, 128, 255")
- with "SVG 1.0 color names" (e.g., "cornflowerblue") which must be specified in lowercase.

6.2.2 Fonts

The fonts GRUB uses "PFF2 font format" bitmap fonts. Fonts are specified with full font names. Currently there is no provision for a preference list of fonts, or deriving one font from another. Fonts are loaded with the "loadfont" command in GRUB. To see the list of loaded fonts, execute the "lsfonts" command. If there are too many fonts to fit on screen, do "set pager=1" before executing "lsfonts".

6.2.3 Progress Bar

Figure 6.1

Figure 6.2

Progress bars are used to display the remaining time before GRUB boots the default menu entry. To create a progress bar that will display the remaining time before automatic boot, simply create a "progress_bar" component with the id "__timeout__". This indicates to GRUB that the progress bar should be updated as time passes, and it should be made invisible if the countdown to automatic boot is interrupted by the user.

Progress bars may optionally have text displayed on them. This text is controlled by variable "text" which contains a printf template with the only argument %d is the number of seconds remaining. Additionally special values "@TIMEOUT_NOTIFICATION_SHORT@", "@TIMEOUT_NOTIFICATION_MIDDLE@", "@TIMEOUT_NOTIFICATION_LONG@" are replaced with standard and translated templates.

6.2.4 Circular Progress Indicator

The circular progress indicator functions similarly to the progress bar. When given an id of "__timeout__", GRUB updates the circular progress indicator's value to indicate the time

remaining. For the circular progress indicator, there are two images used to render it: the
center image, and the *tick* image. The center image is rendered in the center of the
component, while the tick image is used to render each mark along the circumference of the
indicator.

6.2.5 Labels

Text labels can be placed on the boot screen. The font, color, and horizontal alignment can
be specified for labels. If a label is given the id "__timeout__", then the "text" property for
that label is also updated with a message informing the user of the number of seconds remaining until automatic boot. This is useful in case you want the text displayed somewhere
else instead of directly on the progress bar.

6.2.6 Boot Menu

The boot menu where GRUB displays the menu entries from the "grub.cfg" file. It is a
list of items, where each item has a title and an optional icon. The icon is selected based
on the *classes* specified for the menu entry. If there is a PNG file named "myclass.png"
in the "grub/themes/icons" directory, it will be displayed for items which have the class
myclass. The boot menu can be customized in several ways, such as the font and color
used for the menu entry title, and by specifying styled boxes for the menu itself and for the
selected item highlight.

6.2.7 Styled Boxes

One of the most important features for customizing the layout is the use of *styled boxes*.
A styled box is composed of 9 rectangular (and potentially empty) regions, which are used
to seamlessly draw the styled box on screen:

Northwest (nw)	North (n)	Northeast (ne)
West (w)	Center (c)	East (e)
Southwest (sw)	South (s)	Southeast (se)

To support any size of box on screen, the center slice and the slices for the top,
bottom, and sides are all scaled to the correct size for the component on screen, using the
following rules:

1. The edge slices (north, south, east, and west) are scaled in the direction of the edge
   they are adjacent to. For instance, the west slice is scaled vertically.

2. The corner slices (northwest, northeast, southeast, and southwest) are not scaled.

3. The center slice is scaled to fill the remaining space in the middle.

As an example of how an image might be sliced up, consider the styled box used for
a terminal view.

Figure 6.3

6.2.8 Creating Styled Box Images

The Inkscape_ scalable vector graphics editor is a very useful tool for creating styled box
images. One process that works well for slicing a drawing into the necessary image slices is:

1. Create or open the drawing you'd like use.

2. Create a new layer on the top of the layer stack. Make it visible. Select this layer as the current layer.

3. Draw 9 rectangles on your drawing where you'd like the slices to be. Clear the fill option, and set the stroke to 1 pixel wide solid stroke. The corners of the slices must meet precisely; if it is off by a single pixel, it will probably be evident when the styled box is rendered in the GRUB menu. You should probably go to File | Document Properties | Grids and enable a grid or create a guide (click on one of the rulers next to the drawing and drag over the drawing; release the mouse button to place the guide) to help place the rectangles precisely.

4. Right click on the center slice rectangle and choose Object Properties. Change the "Id" to "slice_c" and click Set. Repeat this for the remaining 8 rectangles, giving them Id values of "slice_n", "slice_ne", "slice_e", and so on according to the location.

5. Save the drawing.

6. Select all the slice rectangles. With the slice layer selected, you can simply press Ctrl+A to select all rectangles. The status bar should indicate that 9 rectangles are selected.

7. Click the layer hide icon for the slice layer in the layer palette. The rectangles will remain selected, even though they are hidden.

8. Choose File | Export Bitmap and check the *Batch export 9 selected objects* box. Make sure that *Hide all except selected* is unchecked. click *Export*. This will create PNG files in the same directory as the drawing, named after the slices. These can now be used for a styled box in a GRUB theme.

6.3 Theme File Manual

The theme file is a plain text file. Lines that begin with "#" are ignored and considered comments. (Note: This may not be the case if the previous line ended where a value was expected.)

The theme file contains two types of statements:

1. Global properties.

2. Component construction.

6.3.1 Global Properties

6.3.2 Format

Global properties are specified with the simple format:

- name1: value1
- name2: "value which may contain spaces"
- name3: #88F

In this example, name3 is assigned a color value.

6.3.3 Global Property List

title-text   Specifies the text to display at the top center of the screen as a title.

title-font	Defines the font used for the title message at the top of the screen.
title-color	Defines the color of the title message.
message-font	Defines the font used for messages, such as when GRUB is unable to automatically boot an entry.
message-color	Defines the color of the message text.
message-bg-color	Defines the background color of the message text area.
desktop-image	Specifies the image to use as the background. It will be scaled to fit the screen size.
desktop-color	Specifies the color for the background if *desktop-image* is not specified.
terminal-box	Specifies the file name pattern for the styled box slices used for the command line terminal window. For example, "terminal-box: terminal_*.png" will use the images "terminal_c.png" as the center area, "terminal_n.png" as the north (top) edge, "terminal_nw.png" as the northwest (upper left) corner, and so on. If the image for any slice is not found, it will simply be left empty.

6.3.4 Component Construction

Greater customizability comes is provided by components. A tree of components forms the user interface. *Containers* are components that can contain other components, and there is always a single root component which is an instance of a *canvas* container.

Components are created in the theme file by prefixing the type of component with a '+' sign:

```
+ label { text="GRUB" font="aqui 11" color="#8FF" }
```

properties of a component are specified as "name = value" (whitespace surrounding tokens is optional and is ignored) where *value* may be:

- a single word (e.g., "align = center", "color = #FF8080"),
- a quoted string (e.g., "text = "Hello, World!""), or
- a tuple (e.g., "preferred_size = (120, 80)").

6.3.5 Component List

The following is a list of the components and the properties they support.

- label A label displays a line of text.

  Properties:

text	The text to display.
font	The font to use for text display.
color	The color of the text.
align	The horizontal alignment of the text within the component. Options are "left", "center", and "right".

- image A component that displays an image. The image is scaled to fit the component, although the preferred size defaults to the image's original size unless the "preferred_size" property is explicitly set.

  Properties:

file	The full path to the image file to load.

- progress_bar Displays a horizontally oriented progress bar. It can be rendered using simple solid filled rectangles, or using a pair of pixmap styled boxes.

  Properties:

fg_color	The foreground color for plain solid color rendering.
bg_color	The background color for plain solid color rendering.
border_color	The border color for plain solid color rendering.
text_color	The text color.
show_text	Boolean value indicating whether or not text should be displayed on the progress bar. If set to *false*, then no text will be displayed on the bar. If set to any other value, text will be displayed on the bar.
bar_style	The styled box specification for the frame of the progress bar. Example: "progress_frame_*.png"
highlight_style	The styled box specification for the highlighted region of the progress bar. This box will be used to paint just the highlighted region of the bar, and will be increased in size as the bar nears completion. Example: "progress_hl_*.png".
text	The text to display on the progress bar. If the progress bar's ID is set to "__timeout__", then GRUB will updated this property with an informative message as the timeout approaches.
value	The progress bar current value. Normally not set manually.
start	The progress bar start value. Normally not set manually.
end	The progress bar end value. Normally not set manually.

- circular_progress Displays a circular progress indicator. The appearance of this component is determined by two images: the *center* image and the *tick* image. The center image is generally larger and will be drawn in the center of the component. Around the circumference of a circle within the component, the tick image will be drawn a certain number of times, depending on the properties of the component.

  Properties:

center_bitmap	The file name of the image to draw in the center of the component.
tick_bitmap	The file name of the image to draw for the tick marks.
num_ticks	The number of ticks that make up a full circle.
ticks_disappear	Boolean value indicating whether tick marks should progressively appear, or progressively disappear as *value* approaches *end*. Specify "true" or "false".
value	The progress indicator current value. Normally not set manually.

start   The progress indicator start value. Normally not set
                                           manually.

end   The progress indicator end value. Normally not set
                                           manually.

- boot_menu Displays the GRUB boot menu. It allows selecting items and executing
  them.

  Properties:

item_font   The font to use for the menu item titles.

selected_item_font   The font to use for the selected menu item,
                                           or "inherit" (the default) to use "item_font"
                                           for the selected menu item as well.

item_color   The color to use for the menu item titles.

selected_item_color   The color to use for the selected menu
                                           item, or "inherit" (the default) to use
                                           "item_color" for the selected menu item as
                                           well.

icon_width   The width of menu item icons. Icons are
                                           scaled to the specified size.

icon_height   The height of menu item icons.

item_height   The height of each menu item in pixels.

item_padding   The amount of space in pixels to leave on
                                           each side of the menu item contents.

item_icon_space   The space between an item's icon and the
                                           title text, in pixels.

item_spacing   The amount of space to leave between menu
                                           items, in pixels.

menu_pixmap_style   The image file pattern for the menu frame
                                           styled box. Example: "menu_*.png" (this
                                           will use images such as "menu_c.png",
                                           "menu_w.png", 'menu_nw.png", etc.)

selected_item_pixmap_style   The image file pattern for the selected item
                                           highlight styled box.

scrollbar   Boolean value indicating whether the scroll
                                           bar should be drawn if the frame and thumb
                                           styled boxes are configured.

scrollbar_frame   The image file pattern for the entire scroll
                                           bar. Example: "scrollbar_*.png"

scrollbar_thumb   The image file pattern for the scroll bar
                                           thumb (the part of the scroll bar that moves
                                           as scrolling occurs). Example: "scroll-
                                           bar_thumb_*.png"

max_items_shown   The maximum number of items to show
                                           on the menu. If there are more than
                                           max_items_shown items in the menu, the
                                           list will scroll to make all items accessible.

- canvas Canvas is a container that allows manual placement of components within it. It does not alter the positions of its child components. It assigns all child components their preferred sizes.

- hbox The *hbox* container lays out its children from left to right, giving each one its preferred width. The height of each child is set to the maximum of the preferred heights of all children.

- vbox The *vbox* container lays out its children from top to bottom, giving each one its preferred height. The width of each child is set to the maximum of the preferred widths of all children.

6.3.6 Common properties

The following properties are supported by all components:

'left'   The distance from the left border of container to left border of the object in either of three formats:

x	Value in pixels
p%	Percentage
p%+x	mixture of both

'top'   The distance from the left border of container to left border of the object in same format.

'width'   The width of object in same format.

'height'   The height of object in same format.

'id'   The identifier for the component. This can be any arbitrary string. The ID can be used by scripts to refer to various components in the GUI component tree. Currently, there is one special ID value that GRUB recognizes:

"__timeout__"   Any component with this ID will have its *text*, *start*, *end*, *value*, and *visible* properties set by GRUB when it is counting down to an automatic boot of the default menu entry.

7 Booting GRUB from the network

The following instructions only work on PC BIOS systems where the Preboot eXecution Environment (PXE) is available.

To generate a PXE boot image, run:

```
grub-mkimage --format=i386-pc-pxe --output=grub.pxe --prefix='(pxe)/boot/g
```

Copy 'grub.pxe', '/boot/grub/*.mod', and '/boot/grub/*.lst' to the PXE (TFTP) server, ensuring that '*.mod' and '*.lst' are accessible via the '/boot/grub/' path from the TFTP server root. Set the DHCP server configuration to offer 'grub.pxe' as the boot file (the 'filename' option in ISC dhcpd).

You can also use the grub-mknetdir utility to generate an image and a GRUB directory tree, rather than copying files around manually.

After GRUB has started, files on the TFTP server will be accessible via the '(pxe)' device.

The server and gateway IP address can be controlled by changing the '(pxe)' device name to '(pxe:*server-ip*)' or '(pxe:*server-ip*:*gateway-ip*)'. Note that this should be changed both in the prefix and in any references to the device name in the configuration file.

GRUB provides several environment variables which may be used to inspect or change the behaviour of the PXE device:

'net_pxe_ip'

>The IP address of this machine. Read-only.

'net_pxe_mac'

>The network interface's MAC address. Read-only.

'net_pxe_hostname'

>The client host name provided by DHCP. Read-only.

'net_pxe_domain'

>The client domain name provided by DHCP. Read-only.

'net_pxe_rootpath'

>The path to the client's root disk provided by DHCP. Read-only.

'net_pxe_extensionspath'

>The path to additional DHCP vendor extensions provided by DHCP. Read-only.

'net_pxe_boot_file'

>The boot file name provided by DHCP. Read-only.

'net_pxe_dhcp_server_name'

>The name of the DHCP server responsible for these boot parameters. Read-only.

'net_default_server'

>The default server. Read-write, although setting this is only useful before opening a network device.

8 Using GRUB via a serial line

This chapter describes how to use the serial terminal support in GRUB.

If you have many computers or computers with no display/keyboard, it could be very useful to control the computers through serial communications. To connect one computer with another via a serial line, you need to prepare a null-modem (cross) serial cable, and you may need to have multiport serial boards, if your computer doesn't have extra serial ports. In addition, a terminal emulator is also required, such as minicom. Refer to a manual of your operating system, for more information.

As for GRUB, the instruction to set up a serial terminal is quite simple. Here is an example:

```
grub> serial --unit=0 --speed=9600
grub> terminal_input serial; terminal_output serial
```

The command `serial` initializes the serial unit 0 with the speed 9600bps. The serial unit 0 is usually called 'COM1', so, if you want to use COM2, you must specify '--unit=1' instead. This command accepts many other options, so please refer to Section 14.2.1 [serial], page 54, for more details.

The commands `terminal_input` (see Section 14.2.2 [terminal_input], page 54) and `terminal_output` (see Section 14.2.3 [terminal_output], page 54) choose which type of terminal you want to use. In the case above, the terminal will be a serial terminal, but you can also pass `console` to the command, as 'terminal_input serial console'. In this case, a terminal in which you press any key will be selected as a GRUB terminal. In the example above, note that you need to put both commands on the same command line, as you will lose the ability to type commands on the console after the first command.

However, note that GRUB assumes that your terminal emulator is compatible with VT100 by default. This is true for most terminal emulators nowadays, but you should pass the option '--dumb' to the command if your terminal emulator is not VT100-compatible or implements few VT100 escape sequences. If you specify this option then GRUB provides you with an alternative menu interface, because the normal menu requires several fancy features of your terminal.

9 Using GRUB with vendor power-on keys

Some laptop vendors provide an additional power-on button which boots another OS. GRUB supports such buttons with the 'GRUB_TIMEOUT_BUTTON', 'GRUB_DEFAULT_BUTTON', 'GRUB_HIDDEN_TIMEOUT_BUTTON' and 'GRUB_BUTTON_CMOS_ADDRESS' variables in default/grub (see Section 5.1 [Simple configuration], page 17). 'GRUB_TIMEOUT_BUTTON', 'GRUB_DEFAULT_BUTTON' and 'GRUB_HIDDEN_TIMEOUT_BUTTON' are used instead of the corresponding variables without the '_BUTTON' suffix when powered on using the special button. 'GRUB_BUTTON_CMOS_ADDRESS' is vendor-specific and partially model-specific. Values known to the GRUB team are:

DELL XPS M1530
        85:3

ASUS EEEPC 1005PE
        84:1 (unconfirmed)

To take full advantage of this function, install GRUB into the MBR (see Section 3.1 [Installing GRUB using grub-install], page 9).

If you have a laptop which has a similar feature and not in the above list could you figure your address and contribute? To discover the address do the following:

- boot normally
-
    ```
    sudo modprobe nvram
    sudo cat /dev/nvram | xxd > normal_button.txt
    ```
- boot using vendor button
-
    ```
    sudo modprobe nvram
    sudo cat /dev/nvram | xxd > normal_vendor.txt
    ```

Then compare these text files and find where a bit was toggled. E.g. in case of Dell XPS it was:

    byte 0x47: 20 --> 28

It's a bit number 3 as seen from following table:

0	01
1	02
2	04
3	08
4	10
5	20
6	40
7	80

0x47 is decimal 71. Linux nvram implementation cuts first 14 bytes of CMOS. So the real byte address in CMOS is 71+14=85 So complete address is 85:3

10 GRUB image files

GRUB consists of several images: a variety of bootstrap images for starting GRUB in various ways, a kernel image, and a set of modules which are combined with the kernel image to form a core image. Here is a short overview of them.

'boot.img'

On PC BIOS systems, this image is the first part of GRUB to start. It is written to a master boot record (MBR) or to the boot sector of a partition. Because a PC boot sector is 512 bytes, the size of this image is exactly 512 bytes.

The sole function of 'boot.img' is to read the first sector of the core image from a local disk and jump to it. Because of the size restriction, 'boot.img' cannot understand any file system structure, so grub-setup hardcodes the location of the first sector of the core image into 'boot.img' when installing GRUB.

'diskboot.img'

This image is used as the first sector of the core image when booting from a hard disk. It reads the rest of the core image into memory and starts the kernel. Since file system handling is not yet available, it encodes the location of the core image using a block list format.

'cdboot.img'

This image is used as the first sector of the core image when booting from a CD-ROM drive. It performs a similar function to 'diskboot.img'.

'pxeboot.img'

This image is used as the start of the core image when booting from the network using PXE. See Chapter 7 [Network], page 35.

'lnxboot.img'

This image may be placed at the start of the core image in order to make GRUB look enough like a Linux kernel that it can be booted by LILO using an 'image=' section.

'kernel.img'

This image contains GRUB's basic run-time facilities: frameworks for device and file handling, environment variables, the rescue mode command-line parser, and so on. It is rarely used directly, but is built into all core images.

'core.img'

This is the core image of GRUB. It is built dynamically from the kernel image and an arbitrary list of modules by the grub-mkimage program. Usually, it contains enough modules to access '/boot/grub', and loads everything else (including menu handling, the ability to load target operating systems, and so on) from the file system at run-time. The modular design allows the core image to be kept small, since the areas of disk where it must be installed are often as small as 32KB.

See Section 3.4 [BIOS installation], page 11, for details on where the core image can be installed on PC systems.

'*.mod'   Everything else in GRUB resides in dynamically loadable modules. These are
               often loaded automatically, or built into the core image if they are essential, but
               may also be loaded manually using the `insmod` command (see Section 14.3.22
               [insmod], page 59).

For GRUB Legacy users

GRUB 2 has a different design from GRUB Legacy, and so correspondences with the images
it used cannot be exact. Nevertheless, GRUB Legacy users often ask questions in the terms
they are familiar with, and so here is a brief guide to how GRUB 2's images relate to that.

'stage1'   Stage 1 from GRUB Legacy was very similar to 'boot.img' in GRUB 2, and
               they serve the same function.

'*_stage1_5'
               In GRUB Legacy, Stage 1.5's function was to include enough filesystem code to
               allow the much larger Stage 2 to be read from an ordinary filesystem. In this
               respect, its function was similar to 'core.img' in GRUB 2. However, 'core.img'
               is much more capable than Stage 1.5 was; since it offers a rescue shell, it is
               sometimes possible to recover manually in the event that it is unable to load
               any other modules, for example if partition numbers have changed. 'core.img'
               is built in a more flexible way, allowing GRUB 2 to support reading modules
               from advanced disk types such as LVM and RAID.

               GRUB Legacy could run with only Stage 1 and Stage 2 in some limited config-
               urations, while GRUB 2 requires 'core.img' and cannot work without it.

'stage2'   GRUB 2 has no single Stage 2 image. Instead, it loads modules from
               '/boot/grub' at run-time.

'stage2_eltorito'
               In GRUB 2, images for booting from CD-ROM drives are now constructed
               using 'cdboot.img' and 'core.img', making sure that the core image contains
               the 'iso9660' module. It is usually best to use the `grub-mkrescue` program for
               this.

'nbgrub'   There is as yet no equivalent for 'nbgrub' in GRUB 2; it was used by Etherboot
               and some other network boot loaders.

'pxegrub'   In GRUB 2, images for PXE network booting are now constructed using
               'pxeboot.img' and 'core.img', making sure that the core image contains the
               'pxe' and 'pxecmd' modules. See Chapter 7 [Network], page 35.

11 Filesystem syntax and semantics

GRUB uses a special syntax for specifying disk drives which can be accessed by BIOS. Because of BIOS limitations, GRUB cannot distinguish between IDE, ESDI, SCSI, or others. You must know yourself which BIOS device is equivalent to which OS device. Normally, that will be clear if you see the files in a device or use the command **search** (see Section 14.3.40 [search], page 63).

11.1 How to specify devices

The device syntax is like this:

(*device* [,*partmap-name1 part-num1* [,*partmap-name2 part-num2* [,...]]])

'[]' means the parameter is optional. *device* depends on the disk driver in use. BIOS and EFI disks use either 'fd' or 'hd' followed by a digit, like 'fd0', or 'cd'. AHCI, PATA (ata), crypto, USB use the name of driver followed by a number. Memdisk and host are limited to one disk and so it's refered just by driver name. RAID (md), ofdisk (ieee1275 and nand), LVM (lv), LDM and arcdisk (arc) use intrinsic name of disk prefixed by driver name. Additionally just "nand" refers to the disk aliased as "nand". Conflicts are solved by suffixing a number if necessarry. Commas need to be escaped. Loopback uses whatever name specified to **loopback** command. Hostdisk uses names specified in device.map as long as it's of the form [fhc]d[0-9]* or hostdisk/<OS DEVICE>. For crypto and RAID (md) additionally you can use the syntax <driver name>uuid/<uuid>.

```
(fd0)
(hd0)
(cd)
(ahci0)
(ata0)
(crypto0)
(usb0)
(cryptouuid/123456789abcdef0123456789abcdef0)
(mduuid/123456789abcdef0123456789abcdef0)
(lv/system-root)
(md/myraid)
(md/0)
(ieee1275/disk2)
(ieee1275//pci@1f\,0/ide@d/disk@2)
(nand)
(memdisk)
(host)
(myloop)
(hostdisk//dev/sda)
```

part-num represents the partition number of *device*, starting from one. *partname* is optional but is recommended since disk may have several top-level partmaps. Specifying third and later component you can access to subpartitions.

The syntax '(hd0)' represents using the entire disk (or the MBR when installing GRUB), while the syntax '(hd0,1)' represents using the first partition of the disk (or the boot sector of the partition when installing GRUB).

```
(hd0,msdos1)
(hd0,msdos1,msdos5)
(hd0,msdos1,bsd3)
(hd0,netbsd1)
(hd0,gpt1)
(hd0,1,3)
```

If you enabled the network support, the special drives '(tftp)', '(http)' and so on ars also available. Before using the network drive, you must initialize the network. See Chapter 7 [Network], page 35, for more information.

If you boot GRUB from a CD-ROM, '(cd)' is available. See Section 3.2 [Making a GRUB bootable CD-ROM], page 10, for details.

11.2 How to specify files

There are two ways to specify files, by *absolute file name* and by *block list*.

An absolute file name resembles a Unix absolute file name, using '/' for the directory separator (not '\' as in DOS). One example is '(hd0,1)/boot/grub/grub.cfg'. This means the file '/boot/grub/grub.cfg' in the first partition of the first hard disk. If you omit the device name in an absolute file name, GRUB uses GRUB's *root device* implicitly. So if you set the root device to, say, '(hd1,1)' by the command 'set root=(hd1,1)' (see Section 14.3.42 [set], page 66), then /boot/kernel is the same as (hd1,1)/boot/kernel.

11.3 How to specify block lists

A block list is used for specifying a file that doesn't appear in the filesystem, like a chainloader. The syntax is [offset]+length[,[offset]+length].... Here is an example:

```
0+100,200+1,300+300
```

This represents that GRUB should read blocks 0 through 99, block 200, and blocks 300 through 599. If you omit an offset, then GRUB assumes the offset is zero.

Like the file name syntax (see Section 11.2 [File name syntax], page 44), if a blocklist does not contain a device name, then GRUB uses GRUB's *root device*. So (hd0,2)+1 is the same as +1 when the root device is '(hd0,2)'.

12 GRUB's user interface

GRUB has both a simple menu interface for choosing preset entries from a configuration file, and a highly flexible command-line for performing any desired combination of boot commands.

GRUB looks for its configuration file as soon as it is loaded. If one is found, then the full menu interface is activated using whatever entries were found in the file. If you choose the *command-line* menu option, or if the configuration file was not found, then GRUB drops to the command-line interface.

12.1 The flexible command-line interface

The command-line interface provides a prompt and after it an editable text area much like a command-line in Unix or DOS. Each command is immediately executed after it is entered[1]. The commands (see Section 14.3 [Command-line and menu entry commands], page 55) are a subset of those available in the configuration file, used with exactly the same syntax.

Cursor movement and editing of the text on the line can be done via a subset of the functions available in the Bash shell:

C-F
PC RIGHT KEY
      Move forward one character.

C-B
PC LEFT KEY
      Move back one character.

C-A
HOME   Move to the start of the line.

C-E
END   Move the the end of the line.

C-D
DEL   Delete the character underneath the cursor.

C-H
BS   Delete the character to the left of the cursor.

C-K   Kill the text from the current cursor position to the end of the line.

C-U   Kill backward from the cursor to the beginning of the line.

C-Y   Yank the killed text back into the buffer at the cursor.

C-P
PC UP KEY
      Move up through the history list.

C-N
PC DOWN KEY
      Move down through the history list.

---

[1] However, this behavior will be changed in the future version, in a user-invisible way.

When typing commands interactively, if the cursor is within or before the first word in the command-line, pressing the TAB key (or C-I) will display a listing of the available commands, and if the cursor is after the first word, the TAB will provide a completion listing of disks, partitions, and file names depending on the context. Note that to obtain a list of drives, one must open a parenthesis, as `root (`.

Note that you cannot use the completion functionality in the TFTP filesystem. This is because TFTP doesn't support file name listing for the security.

12.2 The simple menu interface

The menu interface is quite easy to use. Its commands are both reasonably intuitive and described on screen.

Basically, the menu interface provides a list of *boot entries* to the user to choose from. Use the arrow keys to select the entry of choice, then press RET to run it. An optional timeout is available to boot the default entry (the first one if not set), which is aborted by pressing any key.

Commands are available to enter a bare command-line by pressing C (which operates exactly like the non-config-file version of GRUB, but allows one to return to the menu if desired by pressing ESC) or to edit any of the *boot entries* by pressing E.

If you protect the menu interface with a password (see Chapter 22 [Security], page 81), all you can do is choose an entry by pressing RET, or press P to enter the password.

12.3 Editing a menu entry

The menu entry editor looks much like the main menu interface, but the lines in the menu are individual commands in the selected entry instead of entry names.

If an ESC is pressed in the editor, it aborts all the changes made to the configuration entry and returns to the main menu interface.

Each line in the menu entry can be edited freely, and you can add new lines by pressing RET at the end of a line. To boot the edited entry, press CTRL-X.

Although GRUB unfortunately does not support *undo*, you can do almost the same thing by just returning to the main menu using ESC.

13 GRUB environment variables

GRUB supports environment variables which are rather like those offered by all Unix-like systems. Environment variables have a name, which is unique and is usually a short identifier, and a value, which is an arbitrary string of characters. They may be set (see Section 14.3.42 [set], page 66), unset (see Section 14.3.44 [unset], page 66), or looked up (see Section 5.2 [Shell-like scripting], page 21) by name.

A number of environment variables have special meanings to various parts of GRUB. Others may be used freely in GRUB configuration files.

13.1 Special environment variables

These variables have special meaning to GRUB.

13.1.1 biosnum

When chain-loading another boot loader (see Section 4.1.2 [Chain-loading], page 13), GRUB may need to know what BIOS drive number corresponds to the root device (see Section 13.1.29 [root], page 51) so that it can set up registers properly. If the *biosnum* variable is set, it overrides GRUB's own means of guessing this.

For an alternative approach which also changes BIOS drive mappings for the chain-loaded system, see Section 14.3.12 [drivemap], page 57.

13.1.2 chosen

When executing a menu entry, GRUB sets the *chosen* variable to the title of the entry being executed.

If the menu entry is in one or more submenus, then *chosen* is set to the titles of each of the submenus starting from the top level followed by the title of the menu entry itself, separated by '>'.

13.1.3 color_highlight

This variable contains the "highlight" foreground and background terminal colors, separated by a slash ('/'). Setting this variable changes those colors. For the available color names, see Section 13.1.4 [color_normal], page 47.

The default is '`black/white`'.

13.1.4 color_normal

This variable contains the "normal" foreground and background terminal colors, separated by a slash ('/'). Setting this variable changes those colors. Each color must be a name from the following list:

- black
- blue
- green
- cyan
- red

- magenta
- brown
- light-gray
- dark-gray
- light-blue
- light-green
- light-cyan
- light-red
- light-magenta
- yellow
- white

The default is 'white/black'.

13.1.5 debug

This variable may be set to enable debugging output from various components of GRUB. The value is a list of debug facility names separated by whitespace or ',', or 'all' to enable all available debugging output.

13.1.6 default

If this variable is set, it identifies a menu entry that should be selected by default, possibly after a timeout (see Section 13.1.32 [timeout], page 51). The entry may be identified by number or by title.

If the entry is in a submenu, then it must be identified using the titles of each of the submenus starting from the top level followed by the number or title of the menu entry itself, separated by '>'. For example, take the following menu structure:

```
Submenu 1
  Menu Entry 1
  Menu Entry 2
Submenu 2
  Submenu 3
    Menu Entry 3
    Menu Entry 4
  Menu Entry 5
```

"Menu Entry 3" would then be identified as 'Submenu 2>Submenu 3>Menu Entry 3'.

This variable is often set by 'GRUB_DEFAULT' (see Section 5.1 [Simple configuration], page 17), grub-set-default, or grub-reboot.

13.1.7 fallback

If this variable is set, it identifies a menu entry that should be selected if the default menu entry fails to boot. Entries are identified in the same way as for 'default' (see Section 13.1.6 [default], page 48).

13.1.8 gfxmode

If this variable is set, it sets the resolution used on the 'gfxterm' graphical terminal. Note that you can only use modes which your graphics card supports via VESA BIOS Extensions (VBE), so for example native LCD panel resolutions may not be available. The default is 'auto', which selects a platform-specific default that should look reasonable.

The resolution may be specified as a sequence of one or more modes, separated by commas (',') or semicolons (';'); each will be tried in turn until one is found. Each mode should be either 'auto', 'widthxheight', or 'widthxheightxdepth'.

13.1.9 gfxpayload

If this variable is set, it controls the video mode in which the Linux kernel starts up, replacing the 'vga=' boot option (see Section 14.3.24 [linux], page 60). It may be set to 'text' to force the Linux kernel to boot in normal text mode, 'keep' to preserve the graphics mode set using 'gfxmode', or any of the permitted values for 'gfxmode' to set a particular graphics mode (see Section 13.1.8 [gfxmode], page 49).

Depending on your kernel, your distribution, your graphics card, and the phase of the moon, note that using this option may cause GNU/Linux to suffer from various display problems, particularly during the early part of the boot sequence. If you have problems, set this variable to 'text' and GRUB will tell Linux to boot in normal text mode.

The default is platform-specific. On platforms with a native text mode (such as PC BIOS platforms), the default is 'text'. Otherwise the default may be 'auto' or a specific video mode.

This variable is often set by 'GRUB_GFXPAYLOAD_LINUX' (see Section 5.1 [Simple configuration], page 17).

13.1.10 gfxterm_font

If this variable is set, it names a font to use for text on the 'gfxterm' graphical terminal. Otherwise, 'gfxterm' may use any available font.

13.1.11 icondir

If this variable is set, it names a directory in which the GRUB graphical menu should look for icons after looking in the theme's 'icons' directory. See Chapter 6 [Theme file format], page 27.

13.1.12 lang

If this variable is set, it names the language code that the gettext command (see Section 14.3.16 [gettext], page 58) uses to translate strings. For example, French would be named as 'fr', and Simplified Chinese as 'zh_CN'.

grub-mkconfig (see Section 5.1 [Simple configuration], page 17) will try to set a reasonable default for this variable based on the system locale.

13.1.13 locale_dir

If this variable is set, it names the directory where translation files may be found (see Section 14.3.16 [gettext], page 58), usually '/boot/grub/locale'. Otherwise, internationalization is disabled.

grub-mkconfig (see Section 5.1 [Simple configuration], page 17) will set a reasonable default for this variable if internationalization is needed and any translation files are available.

13.1.14 menu_color_highlight

This variable contains the foreground and background colors to be used for the highlighted menu entry, separated by a slash ('/'). Setting this variable changes those colors. For the available color names, see Section 13.1.4 [color_normal], page 47.

The default is the value of 'color_highlight' (see Section 13.1.3 [color_highlight], page 47).

13.1.15 menu_color_normal

This variable contains the foreground and background colors to be used for non-highlighted menu entries, separated by a slash ('/'). Setting this variable changes those colors. For the available color names, see Section 13.1.4 [color_normal], page 47.

The default is the value of 'color_normal' (see Section 13.1.4 [color_normal], page 47).

13.1.16 net_pxe_boot_file

See Chapter 7 [Network], page 35.

13.1.17 net_pxe_dhcp_server_name

See Chapter 7 [Network], page 35.

13.1.18 net_pxe_domain

See Chapter 7 [Network], page 35.

13.1.19 net_pxe_extensionspath

See Chapter 7 [Network], page 35.

13.1.20 net_pxe_hostname

See Chapter 7 [Network], page 35.

13.1.21 net_pxe_ip

See Chapter 7 [Network], page 35.

13.1.22 net_pxe_mac

See Chapter 7 [Network], page 35.

13.1.23 net_pxe_rootpath

See Chapter 7 [Network], page 35.

13.1.24 pager

If set to '1', pause output after each screenful and wait for keyboard input. The default is not to pause output.

13.1.25 prefix

The location of the '/boot/grub' directory as an absolute file name (see Section 11.2 [File name syntax], page 44). This is normally set by GRUB at startup based on information provided by grub-install. GRUB modules are dynamically loaded from this directory, so it must be set correctly in order for many parts of GRUB to work.

13.1.26 pxe_blksize

See Chapter 7 [Network], page 35.

13.1.27 pxe_default_gateway

See Chapter 7 [Network], page 35.

13.1.28 pxe_default_server

See Chapter 7 [Network], page 35.

13.1.29 root

The root device name (see Section 11.1 [Device syntax], page 43). Any file names that do not specify an explicit device name are read from this device. The default is normally set by GRUB at startup based on the value of 'prefix' (see Section 13.1.25 [prefix], page 51).

For example, if GRUB was installed to the first partition of the first hard disk, then 'prefix' might be set to '(hd0,msdos1)/boot/grub' and 'root' to 'hd0,msdos1'.

13.1.30 superusers

This variable may be set to a list of superuser names to enable authentication support. See Chapter 22 [Security], page 81.

13.1.31 theme

This variable may be set to a directory containing a GRUB graphical menu theme. See Chapter 6 [Theme file format], page 27.

This variable is often set by 'GRUB_THEME' (see Section 5.1 [Simple configuration], page 17).

13.1.32 timeout

If this variable is set, it specifies the time in seconds to wait for keyboard input before booting the default menu entry. A timeout of '0' means to boot the default entry immediately without displaying the menu; a timeout of '-1' (or unset) means to wait indefinitely.

This variable is often set by 'GRUB_TIMEOUT' or 'GRUB_HIDDEN_TIMEOUT' (see Section 5.1 [Simple configuration], page 17).

13.2 The GRUB environment block

It is often useful to be able to remember a small amount of information from one boot to the next. For example, you might want to set the default menu entry based on what was selected the last time. GRUB deliberately does not implement support for writing files in order to minimise the possibility of the boot loader being responsible for file system corruption, so a GRUB configuration file cannot just create a file in the ordinary way. However, GRUB provides an "environment block" which can be used to save a small amount of state.

The environment block is a preallocated 1024-byte file, which normally lives in '/boot/grub/grubenv' (although you should not assume this). At boot time, the load_env command (see Section 14.3.27 [load_env], page 60) loads environment variables from it, and the save_env (see Section 14.3.39 [save_env], page 63) command saves environment variables to it. From a running system, the grub-editenv utility can be used to edit the environment block.

For safety reasons, this storage is only available when installed on a plain disk (no LVM or RAID), using a non-checksumming filesystem (no ZFS), and using BIOS or EFI functions (no ATA, USB or IEEE1275).

grub-mkconfig uses this facility to implement 'GRUB_SAVEDEFAULT' (see Section 5.1 [Simple configuration], page 17).

14 The list of available commands

In this chapter, we list all commands that are available in GRUB.

Commands belong to different groups. A few can only be used in the global section of the configuration file (or "menu"); most of them can be entered on the command-line and can be used either anywhere in the menu or specifically in the menu entries.

In rescue mode, only the **insmod** (see Section 14.3.22 [insmod], page 59), **ls** (see Section 14.3.29 [ls], page 61), **set** (see Section 14.3.42 [set], page 66), and **unset** (see Section 14.3.44 [unset], page 66) commands are normally available. If you end up in rescue mode and do not know what to do, then see Section 27.1 [GRUB only offers a rescue shell], page 95.

14.1 The list of commands for the menu only

The semantics used in parsing the configuration file are the following:

- The files *must* be in plain-text format.
- '#' at the beginning of a line in a configuration file means it is only a comment.
- Options are separated by spaces.
- All numbers can be either decimal or hexadecimal. A hexadecimal number must be preceded by '0x', and is case-insensitive.

These commands can only be used in the menu:

14.1.1 menuentry

menuentry *title* ['--class=class'...] ['--users=users']   [Command]
        ['--unrestricted'] ['--hotkey=key'] { *command*; ... }

This defines a GRUB menu entry named *title*. When this entry is selected from the menu, GRUB will set the *chosen* environment variable to *title*, execute the list of commands given within braces, and if the last command in the list returned successfully and a kernel was loaded it will execute the **boot** command.

The '--class' option may be used any number of times to group menu entries into classes. Menu themes may display different classes using different styles.

The '--users' option grants specific users access to specific menu entries. See Chapter 22 [Security], page 81.

The '--unrestricted' option grants all users access to specific menu entries. See Chapter 22 [Security], page 81.

The '--hotkey' option associates a hotkey with a menu entry. *key* may be a single letter, or one of the aliases 'backspace', 'tab', or 'delete'.

14.1.2 submenu

submenu *title* ['--class=class'...] ['--users=users']   [Command]
        ['--unrestricted'] ['--hotkey=key'] { *menu entries* ... }

This defines a submenu. An entry called *title* will be added to the menu; when that entry is selected, a new menu will be displayed showing all the entries within this submenu.

All options are the same as in the `menuentry` command (see Section 14.1.1 [menuentry], page 53).

14.2 The list of general commands

Commands usable anywhere in the menu and in the command-line.

14.2.1 serial

serial ['--unit=unit'] ['--port=port'] ['--speed=speed']   [Command]
       ['--word=word'] ['--parity=parity'] ['--stop=stop']
      Initialize a serial device. *unit* is a number in the range 0-3 specifying which serial
port to use; default is 0, which corresponds to the port often called COM1. *port* is
the I/O port where the UART is to be found; if specified it takes precedence over
unit. *speed* is the transmission speed; default is 9600. *word* and *stop* are the number
of data bits and stop bits. Data bits must be in the range 5-8 and stop bits must be
1 or 2. Default is 8 data bits and one stop bit. *parity* is one of 'no', 'odd', 'even' and
defaults to 'no'.

      The serial port is not used as a communication channel unless the `terminal_input`
or `terminal_output` command is used (see Section 14.2.2 [terminal_input], page 54,
see Section 14.2.3 [terminal_output], page 54).

      See also Chapter 8 [Serial terminal], page 37.

14.2.2 terminal_input

terminal_input ['--append'|'--remove'] [*terminal1*] [*terminal2*] . . .   [Command]
      List or select an input terminal.

      With no arguments, list the active and available input terminals.

      With '--append', add the named terminals to the list of active input terminals; any
of these may be used to provide input to GRUB.

      With '--remove', remove the named terminals from the active list.

      With no options but a list of terminal names, make only the listed terminal names
active.

14.2.3 terminal_output

terminal_output ['--append'|'--remove'] [*terminal1*] [*terminal2*] . . .   [Command]
      List or select an output terminal.

      With no arguments, list the active and available output terminals.

      With '--append', add the named terminals to the list of active output terminals; all
of these will receive output from GRUB.

      With '--remove', remove the named terminals from the active list.

      With no options but a list of terminal names, make only the listed terminal names
active.

14.2.4 terminfo

terminfo [-a|-u|-v] [*term*]   [Command]

> Define the capabilities of your terminal by giving the name of an entry in the terminfo database, which should correspond roughly to a 'TERM' environment variable in Unix.
>
> The currently available terminal types are 'vt100', 'vt100-color', 'ieee1275', and 'dumb'. If you need other terminal types, please contact us to discuss the best way to include support for these in GRUB.
>
> The '-a' ('--ascii'), '-u' ('--utf8'), and '-v' ('--visual-utf8') options control how non-ASCII text is displayed. '-a' specifies an ASCII-only terminal; '-u' specifies logically-ordered UTF-8; and '-v' specifies "visually-ordered UTF-8" (in other words, arranged such that a terminal emulator without bidirectional text support will display right-to-left text in the proper order; this is not really proper UTF-8, but a workaround).
>
> If no option or terminal type is specified, the current terminal type is printed.

14.3 The list of command-line and menu entry commands

These commands are usable in the command-line and in menu entries. If you forget a command, you can run the command **help** (see Section 14.3.19 [help], page 59).

14.3.1 acpi

acpi ['-1'|'-2']   [Command]
        ['--exclude=table1,...'|'--load-only=table1,...'] ['--oemid=id']
        ['--oemtable=table'] ['--oemtablerev=rev']
        ['--oemtablecreator=creator'] ['--oemtablecreatorrev=rev']
        ['--no-ebda'] *filename* ...

> Modern BIOS systems normally implement the Advanced Configuration and Power Interface (ACPI), and define various tables that describe the interface between an ACPI-compliant operating system and the firmware. In some cases, the tables provided by default only work well with certain operating systems, and it may be necessary to replace some of them.
>
> Normally, this command will replace the Root System Description Pointer (RSDP) in the Extended BIOS Data Area to point to the new tables. If the '--no-ebda' option is used, the new tables will be known only to GRUB, but may be used by GRUB's EFI emulation.

14.3.2 badram

badram *addr,mask*[*,addr,mask...*]   [Command]
> Filter out bad RAM.

This command notifies the memory manager that specified regions of RAM ought to be filtered out (usually, because they're damaged). This remains in effect after a payload kernel has been loaded by GRUB, as long as the loaded kernel obtains its memory map from GRUB. Kernels that support this include Linux, GNU Mach, the kernel of FreeBSD and Multiboot kernels in general.

Syntax is the same as provided by the Memtest86+ utility: a list of address/mask pairs. Given a page-aligned address and a base address / mask pair, if all the bits of the page-aligned address that are enabled by the mask match with the base address, it means this page is to be filtered. This syntax makes it easy to represent patterns that are often result of memory damage, due to physical distribution of memory cells.

14.3.3 blocklist

blocklist *file*   [Command]

Print a block list (see Section 11.3 [Block list syntax], page 44) for *file*.

14.3.4 boot

boot   [Command]

Boot the OS or chain-loader which has been loaded. Only necessary if running the fully interactive command-line (it is implicit at the end of a menu entry).

14.3.5 cat

cat ['--dos'] *file*   [Command]

Display the contents of the file *file*. This command may be useful to remind you of your OS's root partition:

    grub> cat /etc/fstab

If the '--dos' option is used, then carriage return / new line pairs will be displayed as a simple new line. Otherwise, the carriage return will be displayed as a control character ('<d>') to make it easier to see when boot problems are caused by a file formatted using DOS-style line endings.

14.3.6 chainloader

chainloader ['--force'] *file*   [Command]

Load *file* as a chain-loader. Like any other file loaded by the filesystem code, it can use the blocklist notation (see Section 11.3 [Block list syntax], page 44) to grab the first sector of the current partition with '+1'. If you specify the option '--force', then load *file* forcibly, whether it has a correct signature or not. This is required when you want to load a defective boot loader, such as SCO UnixWare 7.1.

14.3.7 cmp

cmp *file1* *file2*   [Command]

Compare the file *file1* with the file *file2*. If they differ in size, print the sizes like this:

    Differ in size: 0x1234 [foo], 0x4321 [bar]

If the sizes are equal but the bytes at an offset differ, then print the bytes like this:

    Differ at the offset 777: 0xbe [foo], 0xef [bar]

If they are completely identical, nothing will be printed.

14.3.8 configfile

configfile *file*   [Command]

> Load *file* as a configuration file. If *file* defines any menu entries, then show a menu containing them immediately.

14.3.9 cpuid

cpuid [*-l*]   [Command]

> Check for CPU features. This command is only available on x86 systems.
>
> With the '-l' option, return true if the CPU supports long mode (64-bit).
>
> If invoked without options, this command currently behaves as if it had been invoked with '-l'. This may change in the future.

14.3.10 crc

crc *file*   [Command]

> Display the CRC32 checksum of *file*.

14.3.11 date

date [[*year-*]*month-day*] [*hour:minute*[*:second*]]   [Command]

> With no arguments, print the current date and time.
>
> Otherwise, take the current date and time, change any elements specified as arguments, and set the result as the new date and time. For example, 'date 01-01' will set the current month and day to January 1, but leave the year, hour, minute, and second unchanged.

14.3.12 drivemap

drivemap '-l'|'-r'|['-s'] *from_drive to_drive*   [Command]

> Without options, map the drive *from_drive* to the drive *to_drive*. This is necessary when you chain-load some operating systems, such as DOS, if such an OS resides at a non-first drive. For convenience, any partition suffix on the drive is ignored, so you can safely use ${root} as a drive specification.
>
> With the '-s' option, perform the reverse mapping as well, swapping the two drives.
>
> With the '-l' option, list the current mappings.
>
> With the '-r' option, reset all mappings to the default values.
>
> For example:
>
>   drivemap -s (hd0) (hd1)

14.3.13 echo

echo ['-n'] ['-e'] *string* ...   [Command]

> Display the requested text and, unless the '-n' option is used, a trailing new line. If there is more than one string, they are separated by spaces in the output. As usual in GRUB commands, variables may be substituted using '${var}'.

The '-e' option enables interpretation of backslash escapes. The following sequences are recognised:

\\	backslash
\a	alert (BEL)
\c	suppress trailing new line
\f	form feed
\n	new line
\r	carriage return
\t	horizontal tab
\v	vertical tab

When interpreting backslash escapes, backslash followed by any other character will print that character.

14.3.14 export

export *envvar*   [Command]

Export the environment variable *envvar*. Exported variables are visible to subsidiary configuration files loaded using `configfile`.

14.3.15 false

false   [Command]

Do nothing, unsuccessfully. This is mainly useful in control constructs such as `if` and `while` (see Section 5.2 [Shell-like scripting], page 21).

14.3.16 gettext

gettext *string*   [Command]

Translate *string* into the current language.

The current language code is stored in the 'lang' variable in GRUB's environment (see Section 13.1.12 [lang], page 49). Translation files in MO format are read from 'locale_dir' (see Section 13.1.13 [locale_dir], page 49), usually '/boot/grub/locale'.

14.3.17 gptsync

gptsync *device* [*partition*[+/-[*type*]]] ...   [Command]

Disks using the GUID Partition Table (GPT) also have a legacy Master Boot Record (MBR) partition table for compatibility with the BIOS and with older operating systems. The legacy MBR can only represent a limited subset of GPT partition entries.

This command populates the legacy MBR with the specified *partition* entries on *device*. Up to three partitions may be used.

type is an MBR partition type code; prefix with '0x' if you want to enter this in hexadecimal. The separator between *partition* and *type* may be '+' to make the partition active, or '-' to make it inactive; only one partition may be active. If both the separator and type are omitted, then the partition will be inactive.

14.3.18 halt

halt '--no-apm'   [Command]

> The command halts the computer. If the '--no-apm' option is specified, no APM BIOS call is performed. Otherwise, the computer is shut down using APM.

14.3.19 help

help [*pattern* ...]   [Command]

> Display helpful information about builtin commands. If you do not specify *pattern*, this command shows short descriptions of all available commands.
>
> If you specify any *patterns*, it displays longer information about each of the commands whose names begin with those *patterns*.

14.3.20 initrd

initrd *file*   [Command]

> Load an initial ramdisk for a Linux kernel image, and set the appropriate parameters in the Linux setup area in memory. This may only be used after the linux command (see Section 14.3.24 [linux], page 60) has been run. See also Section 4.3.2 [GNU/Linux], page 14.

14.3.21 initrd16

initrd16 *file*   [Command]

> Load an initial ramdisk for a Linux kernel image to be booted in 16-bit mode, and set the appropriate parameters in the Linux setup area in memory. This may only be used after the linux16 command (see Section 14.3.25 [linux16], page 60) has been run. See also Section 4.3.2 [GNU/Linux], page 14.
>
> This command is only available on x86 systems.

14.3.22 insmod

insmod *module*   [Command]

> Insert the dynamic GRUB module called *module*.

14.3.23 keystatus

keystatus ['--shift'] ['--ctrl'] ['--alt']   [Command]

> Return true if the Shift, Control, or Alt modifier keys are held down, as requested by options. This is useful in scripting, to allow some user control over behaviour without having to wait for a keypress.
>
> Checking key modifier status is only supported on some platforms. If invoked without any options, the keystatus command returns true if and only if checking key modifier status is supported.

14.3.24 linux

linux *file . . .*   [Command]

> Load a Linux kernel image from *file*. The rest of the line is passed verbatim as the
> *kernel command-line*. Any initrd must be reloaded after using this command (see
> Section 14.3.20 [initrd], page 59).
>
> On x86 systems, the kernel will be booted using the 32-bit boot protocol. Note that
> this means that the 'vga=' boot option will not work; if you want to set a special video
> mode, you will need to use GRUB commands such as 'set gfxpayload=1024x768' or
> 'set gfxpayload=keep' (to keep the same mode as used in GRUB) instead. GRUB
> can automatically detect some uses of 'vga=' and translate them to appropriate set-
> tings of 'gfxpayload'. The linux16 command (see Section 14.3.25 [linux16], page 60)
> avoids this restriction.

14.3.25 linux16

linux16 *file . . .*   [Command]

> Load a Linux kernel image from *file* in 16-bit mode. The rest of the line is passed
> verbatim as the *kernel command-line*. Any initrd must be reloaded after using this
> command (see Section 14.3.21 [initrd16], page 59).
>
> The kernel will be booted using the traditional 16-bit boot protocol. As well as
> bypassing problems with 'vga=' described in Section 14.3.24 [linux], page 60, this
> permits booting some other programs that implement the Linux boot protocol for
> the sake of convenience.
>
> This command is only available on x86 systems.

14.3.26 list_env

list_env ['-f' *file*]   [Command]

> List all variables in the environment block file. See Section 13.2 [Environment block],
> page 51.
>
> The '-f' option overrides the default location of the environment block.

14.3.27 load_env

load_env ['-f' *file*]   [Command]

> Load all variables from the environment block file into the environment. See
> Section 13.2 [Environment block], page 51.
>
> The '-f' option overrides the default location of the environment block.

14.3.28 loopback

loopback ['-d'] *device file*   [Command]

> Make the device named *device* correspond to the contents of the filesystem image in
> *file*. For example:
>
> ```
> loopback loop0 /path/to/image
> ls (loop0)/
> ```
>
> With the '-d' option, delete a device previously created using this command.

14.3.29 ls

`ls` [*arg . . .*]   [Command]
    List devices or files.

    With no arguments, print all devices known to GRUB.

    If the argument is a device name enclosed in parentheses (see Section 11.1 [Device syntax], page 43), then list all files at the root directory of that device.

    If the argument is a directory given as an absolute file name (see Section 11.2 [File name syntax], page 44), then list the contents of that directory.

14.3.30 normal

`normal` [*file*]   [Command]
    Enter normal mode and display the GRUB menu.

    In normal mode, commands, filesystem modules, and cryptography modules are automatically loaded, and the full GRUB script parser is available. Other modules may be explicitly loaded using `insmod` (see Section 14.3.22 [insmod], page 59).

    If a *file* is given, then commands will be read from that file. Otherwise, they will be read from '`$prefix/grub.cfg`' if it exists.

    `normal` may be called from within normal mode, creating a nested environment. It is more usual to use `configfile` (see Section 14.3.8 [configfile], page 57) for this.

14.3.31 normal_exit

`normal_exit`   [Command]
    Exit normal mode (see Section 14.3.30 [normal], page 61). If this instance of normal mode was not nested within another one, then return to rescue mode.

14.3.32 parttool

`parttool` *partition commands*   [Command]
    Make various modifications to partition table entries.

    Each *command* is either a boolean option, in which case it must be followed with '`+`' or '`-`' (with no intervening space) to enable or disable that option, or else it takes a value in the form '`command=value`'.

    Currently, `parttool` is only useful on DOS partition tables (also known as Master Boot Record, or MBR). On these partition tables, the following commands are available:

'`boot`' (boolean)
        When enabled, this makes the selected partition be the active (bootable) partition on its disk, clearing the active flag on all other partitions. This command is limited to *primary* partitions.

'`type`' (value)
        Change the type of an existing partition. The value must be a number in the range 0-0xFF (prefix with '`0x`' to enter it in hexadecimal).

'hidden' (boolean)

> When enabled, this hides the selected partition by setting the *hidden* bit in its partition type code; when disabled, unhides the selected partition by clearing this bit. This is useful only when booting DOS or Wwindows and multiple primary FAT partitions exist in one disk. See also Section 4.3.3 [DOS/Windows], page 15.

14.3.33 password

password *user clear-password*   [Command]

> Define a user named *user* with password *clear-password*. See Chapter 22 [Security], page 81.

14.3.34 password_pbkdf2

password_pbkdf2 *user hashed-password*   [Command]

> Define a user named *user* with password hash *hashed-password*. Use grub-mkpasswd-pbkdf2 (see Chapter 30 [Invoking grub-mkpasswd-pbkdf2], page 101) to generate password hashes. See Chapter 22 [Security], page 81.

14.3.35 play

play *file | tempo [pitch1 duration1] [pitch2 duration2] ...*   [Command]
> Plays a tune

> If the argument is a file name (see Section 11.2 [File name syntax], page 44), play the tune recorded in it. The file format is first the tempo as an unsigned 32bit little-endian number, then pairs of unsigned 16bit little-endian numbers for pitch and duration pairs.

> If the arguments are a series of numbers, play the inline tune.

> The tempo is the base for all note durations. 60 gives a 1-second base, 120 gives a half-second base, etc. Pitches are Hz. Set pitch to 0 to produce a rest.

14.3.36 pxe_unload

pxe_unload   [Command]

> Unload the PXE environment (see Chapter 7 [Network], page 35).

> This command is only available on PC BIOS systems.

14.3.37 read

read *[var]*   [Command]

> Read a line of input from the user. If an environment variable *var* is given, set that environment variable to the line of input that was read, with no terminating newline.

14.3.38 reboot

reboot   [Command]

> Reboot the computer.

14.3.39 save_env

save_env ['-f' *file*] var ...   [Command]

> Save the named variables from the environment to the environment block file. See Section 13.2 [Environment block], page 51.

> The '-f' option overrides the default location of the environment block.

14.3.40 search

search ['--file'|'--label'|'--fs-uuid'] ['--set' [*var*]]   [Command]
    ['--no-floppy'] *name*

> Search devices by file ('-f', '--file'), filesystem label ('-l', '--label'), or filesystem UUID ('-u', '--fs-uuid').

> If the '--set' option is used, the first device found is set as the value of environment variable *var*. The default variable is 'root'.

> The '--no-floppy' option prevents searching floppy devices, which can be slow.

> The 'search.file', 'search.fs_label', and 'search.fs_uuid' commands are aliases for 'search --file', 'search --label', and 'search --fs-uuid' respectively.

14.3.41 sendkey

sendkey ['--num'|'--caps'|'--scroll'|'--insert'| [Command]
    '--pause'|'--left-shift'|'--right-shift'|
    '--sysrq'|'--numkey'|'--capskey'|'--scrollkey'|
    '--insertkey'|'--left-alt'|'--right-alt'|
    '--left-ctrl'|'--right-ctrl' 'on'|'off']... ['no-led'] *keystroke*

> Insert keystrokes into the keyboard buffer when booting. Sometimes an operating system or chainloaded boot loader requires particular keys to be pressed: for example, one might need to press a particular key to enter "safe mode", or when chainloading another boot loader one might send keystrokes to it to navigate its menu.

> You may provide up to 16 keystrokes (the length of the BIOS keyboard buffer). Keystroke names may be upper-case or lower-case letters, digits, or taken from the following table:

Name	Key
escape	Escape
exclam	!
at	@
numbersign	#
dollar	$
percent	%
caret	^
ampersand	&
asterisk	*
parenleft	(
parenright	)
minus	-

underscore	_
equal	=
plus	+
backspace	Backspace
tab	Tab
bracketleft	[
braceleft	{
bracketright	]
braceright	}
enter	Enter
control	press and release Control
semicolon	;
colon	:
quote	'
doublequote	"
backquote	'
tilde	~
shift	press and release left Shift
backslash	\
bar		
comma	,
less	<
period	.
greater	>
slash	/
question	?
rshift	press and release right Shift
alt	press and release Alt
space	space bar
capslock	Caps Lock
F1	F1
F2	F2
F3	F3
F4	F4
F5	F5
F6	F6
F7	F7
F8	F8
F9	F9
F10	F10
F11	F11
F12	F12
num1	1 (numeric keypad)
num2	2 (numeric keypad)
num3	3 (numeric keypad)
num4	4 (numeric keypad)
num5	5 (numeric keypad)

num6	6 (numeric keypad)
num7	7 (numeric keypad)
num8	8 (numeric keypad)
num9	9 (numeric keypad)
num0	0 (numeric keypad)
numperiod	. (numeric keypad)
numend	End (numeric keypad)
numdown	Down (numeric keypad)
numpgdown	Page Down (numeric keypad)
numleft	Left (numeric keypad)
numcenter	5 with Num Lock inactive (numeric keypad)
numright	Right (numeric keypad)
numhome	Home (numeric keypad)
numup	Up (numeric keypad)
numpgup	Page Up (numeric keypad)
numinsert	Insert (numeric keypad)
numdelete	Delete (numeric keypad)
numasterisk	* (numeric keypad)
numminus	- (numeric keypad)
numplus	+ (numeric keypad)
numslash	/ (numeric keypad)
numenter	Enter (numeric keypad)
delete	Delete
insert	Insert
home	Home
end	End
pgdown	Page Down
pgup	Page Up
down	Down
up	Up
left	Left
right	Right

As well as keystrokes, the **sendkey** command takes various options that affect the BIOS keyboard status flags. These options take an 'on' or 'off' parameter, specifying that the corresponding status flag be set or unset; omitting the option for a given status flag will leave that flag at its initial state at boot. The '--num', '--caps', '--scroll', and '--insert' options emulate setting the corresponding mode, while the '--numkey', '--capskey', '--scrollkey', and '--insertkey' options emulate pressing and holding the corresponding key. The other status flag options are self-explanatory.

If the '--no-led' option is given, the status flag options will have no effect on keyboard LEDs.

If the **sendkey** command is given multiple times, then only the last invocation has any effect.

Since `sendkey` manipulates the BIOS keyboard buffer, it may cause hangs, reboots, or other misbehaviour on some systems. If the operating system or boot loader that runs after GRUB uses its own keyboard driver rather than the BIOS keyboard functions, then `sendkey` will have no effect.

This command is only available on PC BIOS systems.

14.3.42 set

set [*envvar=value*]   [Command]
Set the environment variable *envvar* to *value*. If invoked with no arguments, print all environment variables with their values.

14.3.43 true

true   [Command]
Do nothing, successfully. This is mainly useful in control constructs such as `if` and `while` (see Section 5.2 [Shell-like scripting], page 21).

14.3.44 unset

unset *envvar*   [Command]
Unset the environment variable *envvar*.

14.3.45 uppermem

This command is not yet implemented for GRUB 2, although it is planned.

15 Charset

GRUB uses UTF-8 internally other than in rendering where some GRUB-specific appropriate representation is used. All text files (including config) are assumed to be encoded in UTF-8.

16 Filesystems

NTFS, JFS, UDF, HFS+, exFAT, long filenames in FAT, Joliet part of ISO9660 are treated as UTF-16 as per specification. AFS and BFS are read as UTF-8, again according to specification. BtrFS, cpio, tar, squash4, minix, minix2, minix3, ROMFS, ReiserFS, XFS, ext2, ext3, ext4, FAT (short names), RockRidge part of ISO9660, nilfs2, UFS1, UFS2 and ZFS are assumed to be UTF-8. This might be false on systems configured with legacy charset but as long as the charset used is superset of ASCII you should be able to access ASCII-named files. And it's recommended to configure your system to use UTF-8 to access the filesystem, convmv may help with migration. ISO9660 (plain) filenames are specified as being ASCII or being described with unspecified escape sequences. GRUB assumes that the ISO9660 names are UTF-8 (since any ASCII is valid UTF-8). There are some old CD-ROMs which use CP437 in non-compliant way. You're still able to access files with names containing only ASCII characters on such filesystems though. You're also able to access any file if the filesystem contains valid Joliet (UTF-16) or RockRidge (UTF-8). AFFS, SFS and HFS never use unicode and GRUB assumes them to be in Latin1, Latin1 and MacRoman respectively. GRUB handles filesystem case-insensitivity however no attempt is performed at case conversion of international characters so e.g. a file named lowercase greek alpha is treated as different from the one named as uppercase alpha. The filesystems in questions are NTFS (except POSIX namespace), HFS+ (configurable at mkfs time, default insensitive), SFS (configurable at mkfs time, default insensitive), JFS (configurable at mkfs time, default sensitive), HFS, AFFS, FAT, exFAT and ZFS (configurable on per-subvolume basis by property "casesensitivity", default sensitive). On ZFS subvolumes marked as case insensitive files containing lowercase international characters are inaccessible. Also like all supported filesystems except HFS+ and ZFS (configurable on per-subvolume basis by property "normalization", default none) GRUB makes no attempt at check of canonical equivalence so a file name u-diaresis is treated as distinct from u+combining diaresis. This however means that in order to access file on HFS+ its name must be specified in normalisation form D. On normalized ZFS subvolumes filenames out of normalisation are inaccessible.

17 Output terminal

Firmware output console "console" on ARC and IEEE1275 are limited to ASCII. BIOS firmware console and VGA text are limited to ASCII and some pseudographics. None of above mentioned is appropriate for displaying international and any unsupported character is replaced with question mark except pseudographics which we attempt to approximate with ASCII. EFI console on the other hand nominally supports UTF-16 but actual language coverage depends on firmware and may be very limited. The encoding used on serial can be chosen with `terminfo` as either ASCII, UTF-8 or "visual UTF-8". Last one is against the specification but results in correct rendering of right-to-left on some readers which don't have own bidi implementation. When using gfxterm or gfxmenu GRUB itself is responsible for rendering the text. In this case GRUB is limited by loaded fonts. If fonts contain all required characters then bidirectional text, cursive variants and combining marks other than enclosing, half (e.g. left half tilde or combining overline) and double ones. Ligatures aren't supported though. This should cover European, Middle Eastern (if you don't mind lack of lam-alif ligature in Arabic) and East Asian scripts. Notable unsupported scripts are Brahmic family and derived as well as Mongolian, Tifinagh, Korean Jamo (precomposed characters have no problem) and tonal writing (2e5-2e9). GRUB also ignores deprecated (as specified in Unicode) characters (e.g. tags). GRUB also doesn't handle so called "annotation characters" If you can complete either of two lists or, better, propose a patch to improve rendering, please contact developper team.

18 Input terminal

Firmware console on BIOS, IEEE1275 and ARC doesn't allow you to enter non-ASCII characters. EFI specification allows for such but author is unaware of any actual implementations. Serial input is currently limited for latin1 (unlikely to change). Own keyboard implementations (at_keyboard and usb_keyboard) supports any key but work on one-char-per-keystroke. So no dead keys or advanced input method. Also there is no keymap change hotkey. In practice it makes difficult to enter any text using non-Latin alphabet. Moreover all current input consumers are limited to ASCII.

19 Gettext

GRUB supports being translated. For this you need to have language *.mo files in $prefix/locale, load gettext module and set "lang" variable.

20 Regexp

Regexps work on unicode characters, however no attempt at checking cannonical equivalence has been made. Moreover the classes like [:alpha:] match only ASCII subset.

21 Other

Currently GRUB always uses YEAR-MONTH-DAY HOUR:MINUTE:SECOND [WEEK-DAY] 24-hour datetime format but weekdays are translated. GRUB always uses the decimal number format with [0-9] as digits and . as descimal separator and no group separator. IEEE1275 aliases are matched case-insensitively except non-ASCII which is matched as binary. Similar behaviour is for matching OSBundleRequired. Since IEEE1275 aliases and OSBundleRequired don't contain any non-ASCII it should never be a problem in practice. Case-sensitive identifiers are matched as raw strings, no canonical equivalence check is performed. Case-insenstive identifiers are matched as RAW but additionally [a-z] is equivalent to [A-Z]. GRUB-defined identifiers use only ASCII and so should user-defined ones. Identifiers containing non-ASCII may work but aren't supported. Only the ASCII space characters (space U+0020, tab U+000b, CR U+000d and LF U+000a) are recognised. Other unicode space characters aren't a valid field separator. test tests <, >, <=, >=, -pgt and -plt compare the strings in the lexicographical order of unicode codepoints, replicating the behaviour of test from coreutils. environment variables and commands are listed in the same order.

22 Authentication and authorisation

By default, the boot loader interface is accessible to anyone with physical access to the console: anyone can select and edit any menu entry, and anyone can get direct access to a GRUB shell prompt. For most systems, this is reasonable since anyone with direct physical access has a variety of other ways to gain full access, and requiring authentication at the boot loader level would only serve to make it difficult to recover broken systems.

However, in some environments, such as kiosks, it may be appropriate to lock down the boot loader to require authentication before performing certain operations.

The 'password' (see Section 14.3.33 [password], page 62) and 'password_pbkdf2' (see Section 14.3.34 [password_pbkdf2], page 62) commands can be used to define users, each of which has an associated password. 'password' sets the password in plain text, requiring 'grub.cfg' to be secure; 'password_pbkdf2' sets the password hashed using the Password-Based Key Derivation Function (RFC 2898), requiring the use of grub-mkpasswd-pbkdf2 (see Chapter 30 [Invoking grub-mkpasswd-pbkdf2], page 101) to generate password hashes.

In order to enable authentication support, the 'superusers' environment variable must be set to a list of usernames, separated by any of spaces, commas, semicolons, pipes, or ampersands. Superusers are permitted to use the GRUB command line, edit menu entries, and execute any menu entry. If 'superusers' is set, then use of the command line is automatically restricted to superusers.

Other users may be given access to specific menu entries by giving a list of usernames (as above) using the '--users' option to the 'menuentry' command (see Section 14.1.1 [menuentry], page 53). If the '--unrestricted' option is used for a menu entry, then that entry is unrestricted. If the '--users' option is not used for a menu entry, then that only superusers are able to use it.

Putting this together, a typical 'grub.cfg' fragment might look like this:

```
set superusers="root"
password_pbkdf2 root grub.pbkdf2.sha512.10000.biglongstring
password user1 insecure

menuentry "May be run by any user" --unrestricted {
set root=(hd0,1)
linux /vmlinuz
}

menuentry "Superusers only" --users "" {
set root=(hd0,1)
linux /vmlinuz single
}

menuentry "May be run by user1 or a superuser" --users user1 {
set root=(hd0,2)
chainloader +1
}
```

The grub-mkconfig program does not yet have built-in support for generating configuration files with authentication. You can use '/etc/grub.d/40_custom' to add simple superuser authentication, by adding *set superusers=* and *password* or *password_pbkdf2* commands.

23 Platform limitations

GRUB2 is designed to be portable and is actually ported across platforms. We try to keep all platforms at the level. Unfortunately some platforms are better supported than others. This is detailed in current and 2 following sections.

ARC platform is unable to change datetime (firmware doesn't seem to provide a function for it). EMU has similar limitation.

ARC platform no serial port is available. EMU has similar limitation.

Console charset refers only to firmware-assisted console. gfxterm is always Unicode (see Internationalisation section for its limitations). Serial is configurable to UTF-8 or ASCII (see Internationalisation). In case of qemu and coreboot ports the refered console is vga_text. Loongson always uses gfxterm.

Most limited one is ASCII. CP437 provides additionally pseudographics. GRUB2 doesn't use any language characters from CP437 as often CP437 is replaced by national encoding compatible only in pseudographics. Unicode is the most versatile charset which supports many languages. However the actual console may be much more limited depending on firmware

On BIOS network is supported only if the image is loaded through network. On sparc64 GRUB is unable to determine which server it was booted from.

On platforms not having direct serial support (as indicated in the line serial) you can still redirect firmware console to serial if it allows so.

Direct ATA/AHCI support allows to circumvent various firmware limitations but isn't needed for normal operation except on baremetal ports.

AT keyboard support allows keyboard layout remapping and support for keys not available through firmware. It isn't needed for normal operation except baremetal ports.

USB support provides benefits similar to ATA (for USB disks) or AT (for USB keyboards). In addition it allows USBserial.

Chainloading refers to the ability to load another bootloader through the same protocol

Hints allow faster disk discovery by already knowing in advance which is the disk in question. On some platforms hints are correct unless you move the disk between boots. On other platforms it's just an educated guess. Note that hint failure results in just reduced performance, not a failure

BadRAM is the ability to mark some of the RAM as "bad". Note: due to protocol limitations mips-loongson (with Linux protocol) and mips-qemu_mips can use only memory up to first hole.

	BIOS	Coreboot	Multiboot	Qemu
video	yes	yes	yes	yes
console charset	CP437	CP437	CP437	CP437
network	yes (*)	no	no	no
ATA/AHCI	yes	yes	yes	yes
AT keyboard	yes	yes	yes	yes
USB	yes	yes	yes	yes
chainloader	local	yes	yes	no

cpuid	partial	partial	partial	partial
hints	guess	guess	guess	guess
PCI	yes	yes	yes	yes
badram	yes	yes	yes	yes
compression	always	pointless	no	no
exit	yes	no	no	no

	ia32 EFI	amd64 EFI	ia32 IEEE1275	Itanium
video	yes	yes	no	no
console charset	Unicode	Unicode	ASCII	Unicode
network	yes	yes	yes	yes
ATA/AHCI	yes	yes	yes	no
AT keyboard	yes	yes	yes	no
USB	yes	yes	yes	no
chainloader	local	local	no	local
cpuid	partial	partial	partial	no
hints	guess	guess	good	guess
PCI	yes	yes	yes	no
badram	yes	yes	no	yes
compression	no	no	no	no
exit	yes	yes	yes	yes

	Loongson	sparc64	Powerpc	ARC
video	yes	no	yes	no
console charset	N/A	ASCII	ASCII	ASCII
network	no	yes (*)	yes	no
ATA/AHCI	yes	no	no	no
AT keyboard	yes	no	no	no
USB	yes	no	no	no
chainloader	yes	no	no	no
cpuid	no	no	no	no
hints	good	good	good	no
PCI	yes	no	no	no
badram	yes (*)	no	no	no
compression	configurable	no	no	configurable
exit	no	yes	yes	yes

	MIPS qemu	emu
video	no	yes
console charset	CP437	ASCII
network	no	yes
ATA/AHCI	yes	no
AT keyboard	yes	no
USB	N/A	yes
chainloader	yes	no
cpuid	no	no
hints	guess	no
PCI	no	no
badram	yes (*)	no

compression	configurable	no
exit	no	yes

24 Outline

Some platforms have features which allows to implement some commands useless or not implementable on others.

Quick summary:

Information retrieval:

- mipsel-loongson: lsspd
- mips-arc: lsdev
- efi: lsefisystab, lssal, lsefimmap
- i386-pc: lsapm
- acpi-enabled (i386-pc, i386-coreboot, i386-multiboot, *-efi): lsacpi

Workarounds for platform-specific issues:

- i386-efi/x86_64-efi: loadbios, fixvideo
- acpi-enabled (i386-pc, i386-coreboot, i386-multiboot, *-efi): acpi (override ACPI tables)
- i386-pc: drivemap
- i386-pc: sendkey

Advanced operations for power users:

- x86: iorw (direct access to I/O ports)

Miscelaneous:

- cmos (x86-*, ieee1275, mips-qemu_mips, mips-loongson): cmostest (used on some laptops to check for special power-on key)
- i386-pc: play

25 Supported boot targets

X86 support is summarised in the following table. "Yes" means that the kernel works on the given platform, "crashes" means an early kernel crash which we hope will be fixed by concerned kernel developers. "no" means GRUB doesn't load the given kernel on a given platform. "headless" means that the kernel works but lacks console drivers (you can still use serial or network console). In case of "no" and "crashes" the reason is given in footnote.

	BIOS	Coreboot
BIOS chainloading	yes	no (1)
NTLDR	yes	no (1)
Plan9	yes	no (1)
Freedos	yes	no (1)
FreeBSD bootloader	yes	crashes (1)
32-bit kFreeBSD	yes	crashes (2,6)
64-bit kFreeBSD	yes	crashes (2,6)
32-bit kNetBSD	yes	crashes (1)
64-bit kNetBSD	yes	crashes (2)
32-bit kOpenBSD	yes	yes
64-bit kOpenBSD	yes	yes
Multiboot	yes	yes
Multiboot2	yes	yes
32-bit Linux (legacy protocol)	yes	no (1)
64-bit Linux (legacy protocol)	yes	no (1)
32-bit Linux (modern protocol)	yes	yes
64-bit Linux (modern protocol)	yes	yes
32-bit XNU	yes	?
64-bit XNU	yes	?
32-bit EFI chainloader	no (3)	no (3)
64-bit EFI chainloader	no (3)	no (3)
Appleloader	no (3)	no (3)

	Multiboot	Qemu
BIOS chainloading	no (1)	no (1)
NTLDR	no (1)	no (1)
Plan9	no (1)	no (1)
FreeDOS	no (1)	no (1)
FreeBSD bootloader	crashes (1)	crashes (1)
32-bit kFreeBSD	crashes (6)	crashes (6)
64-bit kFreeBSD	crashes (6)	crashes (6)
32-bit kNetBSD	crashes (1)	crashes (1)
64-bit kNetBSD	yes	yes
32-bit kOpenBSD	yes	yes
64-bit kOpenBSD	yes	yes
Multiboot	yes	yes
Multiboot2	yes	yes
32-bit Linux (legacy protocol)	no (1)	no (1)
64-bit Linux (legacy protocol)	no (1)	no (1)

32-bit Linux (modern protocol)	yes	yes
64-bit Linux (modern protocol)	yes	yes
32-bit XNU	?	?
64-bit XNU	?	?
32-bit EFI chainloader	no (3)	no (3)
64-bit EFI chainloader	no (3)	no (3)
Appleloader	no (3)	no (3)
	ia32 EFI	amd64 EFI
BIOS chainloading	no (1)	no (1)
NTLDR	no (1)	no (1)
Plan9	no (1)	no (1)
FreeDOS	no (1)	no (1)
FreeBSD bootloader	crashes (1)	crashes (1)
32-bit kFreeBSD	headless	headless
64-bit kFreeBSD	headless	headless
32-bit kNetBSD	crashes (1)	crashes (1)
64-bit kNetBSD	yes	yes
32-bit kOpenBSD	headless	headless
64-bit kOpenBSD	headless	headless
Multiboot	yes	yes
Multiboot2	yes	yes
32-bit Linux (legacy protocol)	no (1)	no (1)
64-bit Linux (legacy protocol)	no (1)	no (1)
32-bit Linux (modern protocol)	yes	yes
64-bit Linux (modern protocol)	yes	yes
32-bit XNU	yes	yes
64-bit XNU	yes (5)	yes
32-bit EFI chainloader	yes	no (4)
64-bit EFI chainloader	no (4)	yes
Appleloader	yes	yes
	ia32 IEEE1275	
BIOS chainloading	no (1)	
NTLDR	no (1)	
Plan9	no (1)	
FreeDOS	no (1)	
FreeBSD bootloader	crashes (1)	
32-bit kFreeBSD	crashes (6)	
64-bit kFreeBSD	crashes (6)	
32-bit kNetBSD	crashes (1)	
64-bit kNetBSD	?	
32-bit kOpenBSD	?	
64-bit kOpenBSD	?	
Multiboot	?	
Multiboot2	?	
32-bit Linux (legacy protocol)	no (1)	
64-bit Linux (legacy protocol)	no (1)	

32-bit Linux (modern protocol)	?
64-bit Linux (modern protocol)	?
32-bit XNU	?
64-bit XNU	?
32-bit EFI chainloader	no (3)
64-bit EFI chainloader	no (3)
Appleloader	no (3)

1. Requires BIOS

2. Crashes because the memory at 0x0-0x1000 isn't available

3. EFI only

4. 32-bit and 64-bit EFI have different structures and work in different CPU modes so it's not possible to chainload 32-bit bootloader on 64-bit platform and vice-versa

5. Some modules may need to be disabled

6. Requires ACPI

PowerPC, IA64 and Sparc64 ports support only Linux. MIPS port supports Linux and multiboot2.

26 Boot tests

As you have seen in previous chapter the support matrix is pretty big and some of the configurations are only rarely used. To ensure the quality bootchecks are available for all x86 targets except EFI chainloader, Appleloader and XNU. All x86 platforms have bootcheck facility except ieee1275. Multiboot, multiboot2, BIOS chainloader, ntldr and freebsd-bootloader boot targets are tested only with a fake kernel images. Only Linux is tested among the payloads using Linux protocols.

Following variables must be defined:

GRUB_PAYLOADS_DIR	directory containing the required kernels
GRUB_CBFSTOOL	cbfstoll from Coreboot package (for coreboot platform only)
GRUB_COREBOOT_ROM	empty Coreboot ROM
GRUB_QEMU_OPTS	additional options to be supplied to QEMU

Required files are:

kfreebsd_env.i386	32-bit kFreeBSD device hints
kfreebsd.i386	32-bit FreeBSD kernel image
kfreebsd.x86_64,	same from 64-bit kFreeBSD
kfreebsd_env.x86_64	
knetbsd.i386	32-bit NetBSD kernel image
knetbsd.miniroot.i386	32-bit kNetBSD miniroot.kmod.
knetbsd.x86_64,	same from 64-bit kNetBSD
knetbsd.miniroot.x86_64	
kopenbsd.i386	32-bit OpenBSD kernel bsd.rd image
kopenbsd.x86_64	same from 64-bit kOpenBSD
linux.i386	32-bit Linux
linux.x86_64	64-bit Linux

27 Error messages produced by GRUB

27.1 GRUB only offers a rescue shell

GRUB's normal start-up procedure involves setting the 'prefix' environment variable to a value set in the core image by grub-install, setting the 'root' variable to match, loading the 'normal' module from the prefix, and running the 'normal' command (see Section 14.3.30 [normal], page 61). This command is responsible for reading '/boot/grub/grub.cfg', running the menu, and doing all the useful things GRUB is supposed to do.

If, instead, you only get a rescue shell, this usually means that GRUB failed to load the 'normal' module for some reason. It may be possible to work around this temporarily: for instance, if the reason for the failure is that 'prefix' is wrong (perhaps it refers to the wrong device, or perhaps the path to '/boot/grub' was not correctly made relative to the device), then you can correct this and enter normal mode manually:

```
# Inspect the current prefix (and other preset variables):
set
# Find out which devices are available:
ls
# Set to the correct value, which might be something like this:
set prefix=(hd0,1)/grub
set root=(hd0,1)
insmod normal
normal
```

However, any problem that leaves you in the rescue shell probably means that GRUB was not correctly installed. It may be more useful to try to reinstall it properly using **grub-install device** (see Chapter 28 [Invoking grub-install], page 97). When doing this, there are a few things to remember:

- Drive ordering in your operating system may not be the same as the boot drive ordering used by your firmware. Do not assume that your first hard drive (e.g. '/dev/sda') is the one that your firmware will boot from. 'device.map' (see Section 3.3 [Device map], page 10) can be used to override this, but it is usually better to use UUIDs or file system labels and avoid depending on drive ordering entirely.

- At least on BIOS systems, if you tell grub-install to install GRUB to a partition but GRUB has already been installed in the master boot record, then the GRUB installation in the partition will be ignored.

- If possible, it is generally best to avoid installing GRUB to a partition (unless it is a special partition for the use of GRUB alone, such as the BIOS Boot Partition used on GPT). Doing this means that GRUB may stop being able to read its core image due to a file system moving blocks around, such as while defragmenting, running checks, or even during normal operation. Installing to the whole disk device is normally more robust.

- Check that GRUB actually knows how to read from the device and file system containing '/boot/grub'. It will not be able to read from encrypted devices, nor from file systems for which support has not yet been added to GRUB.

28 Invoking grub-install

The program `grub-install` installs GRUB on your drive using `grub-mkimage` and (on some platforms) `grub-setup`. You must specify the device name on which you want to install GRUB, like this:

    grub-install install_device

The device name *install_device* is an OS device name or a GRUB device name.

`grub-install` accepts the following options:

'`--help`'   Print a summary of the command-line options and exit.

'`--version`'

Print the version number of GRUB and exit.

'`--boot-directory=dir`'

Install GRUB images under the directory '`dir/grub/`' This option is useful when you want to install GRUB into a separate partition or a removable disk. If this option is not specified then it defaults to '`/boot`', so

    grub-install /dev/sda

is equivalent to

    grub-install --boot-directory=/boot/ /dev/sda

Here is an example in which you have a separate *boot* partition which is mounted on '`/mnt/boot`':

    grub-install --boot-directory=/mnt/boot /dev/sdb

'`--recheck`'

Recheck the device map, even if '`/boot/grub/device.map`' already exists. You should use this option whenever you add/remove a disk into/from your computer.

29 Invoking grub-mkconfig

The program `grub-mkconfig` generates a configuration file for GRUB (see Section 5.1 [Simple configuration], page 17).

    grub-mkconfig -o /boot/grub/grub.cfg

`grub-mkconfig` accepts the following options:

'`--help`'   Print a summary of the command-line options and exit.

'`--version`'
          Print the version number of GRUB and exit.

'`-o file`'
'`--output=file`'
          Send the generated configuration file to *file*. The default is to send it to standard output.

30 Invoking grub-mkpasswd-pbkdf2

The program `grub-mkpasswd-pbkdf2` generates password hashes for GRUB (see Chapter 22 [Security], page 81).

> `grub-mkpasswd-pbkdf2`
>
> `grub-mkpasswd-pbkdf2` accepts the following options:

'`-c` *number*'
'`--iteration-count=`*number*'
> Number of iterations of the underlying pseudo-random function. Defaults to 10000.

'`-l` *number*'
'`--buflen=`*number*'
> Length of the generated hash. Defaults to 64.

'`-s` *number*'
'`--salt=`*number*'
> Length of the salt. Defaults to 64.

31 Invoking grub-mkrescue

The program `grub-mkrescue` generates a bootable GRUB rescue image (see Section 3.2 [Making a GRUB bootable CD-ROM], page 10).

        grub-mkrescue -o grub.iso

All arguments not explicitly listed as `grub-mkrescue` options are passed on directly to `xorriso` in `mkisofs` emulation mode. Options passed to `xorriso` will normally be interpreted as `mkisofs` options; if the option '`--`' is used, then anything after that will be interpreted as native `xorriso` options.

Non-option arguments specify additional source directories. This is commonly used to add extra files to the image:

        mkdir -p disk/boot/grub
        (add extra files to 'disk/boot/grub')
        grub-mkrescue -o grub.iso disk

`grub-mkrescue` accepts the following options:

'`--help`' Print a summary of the command-line options and exit.

'`--version`'
        Print the version number of GRUB and exit.

'`-o file`'
'`--output=file`'
        Save output in *file*. This "option" is required.

'`--modules=modules`'
        Pre-load the named GRUB modules in the image. Multiple entries in *modules* should be separated by whitespace (so you will probably need to quote this for your shell).

'`--rom-directory=dir`'
        If generating images for the QEMU or Coreboot platforms, copy the resulting '`qemu.img`' or '`coreboot.elf`' files respectively to the *dir* directory as well as including them in the image.

'`--xorriso=file`'
        Use *file* as the `xorriso` program, rather than the built-in default.

'`--grub-mkimage=file`'
        Use *file* as the `grub-mkimage` program, rather than the built-in default.

32 Invoking grub-probe

The program `grub-probe` probes device information for a given path or device.

```
grub-probe --target=fs /boot/grub
grub-probe --target=drive --device /dev/sda1
```

`grub-probe` must be given a path or device as a non-option argument, and also accepts the following options:

`--help`   Print a summary of the command-line options and exit.

`--version`

> Print the version number of GRUB and exit.

`-d`
`--device`

> If this option is given, then the non-option argument is a system device name (such as '`/dev/sda1`'), and `grub-probe` will print information about that device. If it is not given, then the non-option argument is a filesystem path (such as '`/boot/grub`'), and `grub-probe` will print information about the device containing that part of the filesystem.

`-m file`
`--device-map=file`

> Use *file* as the device map (see Section 3.3 [Device map], page 10) rather than the default, usually '`/boot/grub/device.map`'.

`-t target`
`--target=target`

> Print information about the given path or device as defined by *target*. The available targets and their meanings are:

> `fs`   GRUB filesystem module.

> `fs_uuid`   Filesystem Universally Unique Identifier (UUID).

> `fs_label`
> > Filesystem label.

> `drive`   GRUB device name.

> `device`   System device name.

> `partmap`   GRUB partition map module.

> `abstraction`
> > GRUB abstraction module (e.g. '`lvm`').

> `cryptodisk_uuid`
> > Crypto device UUID.

> `msdos_parttype`
> > MBR partition type code (two hexadecimal digits).

> `hints_string`
> > A string of platform search hints suitable for passing to the **search** command (see Section 14.3.40 [search], page 63).

‘bios_hints’

Search hints for the PC BIOS platform.

‘ieee1275_hints’

Search hints for the IEEE1275 platform.

‘baremetal_hints’

Search hints for platforms where disks are addressed directly rather than via firmware.

‘efi_hints’

Search hints for the EFI platform.

‘arc_hints’

Search hints for the ARC platform.

‘compatibility_hint’

A guess at a reasonable GRUB drive name for this device, which may be used as a fallback if the **search** command fails.

‘disk’   System device name for the whole disk.

‘-v’
‘--verbose’

Print verbose messages.

Appendix A How to obtain and build GRUB

Caution: GRUB requires binutils-2.9.1.0.23 or later because the GNU assembler has been changed so that it can produce real 16bits machine code between 2.9.1 and 2.9.1.0.x. See `http://sources.redhat.com/binutils/`, to obtain information on how to get the latest version.

GRUB is available from the GNU alpha archive site `ftp://ftp.gnu.org/gnu/grub` or any of its mirrors. The file will be named grub-version.tar.gz. The current version is 2.00, so the file you should grab is:

`ftp://ftp.gnu.org/gnu/grub/grub-2.00.tar.gz`

To unbundle GRUB use the instruction:

`zcat grub-2.00.tar.gz | tar xvf -`

which will create a directory called '`grub-2.00`' with all the sources. You can look at the file '`INSTALL`' for detailed instructions on how to build and install GRUB, but you should be able to just do:

```
cd grub-2.00
./configure
make install
```

Also, the latest version is available using Bazaar. See `http://www.gnu.org/software/grub` for more information.

Appendix B Reporting bugs

These are the guideline for how to report bugs. Take a look at this list below before you submit bugs:

1. Before getting unsettled, read this manual through and through. Also, see the GNU GRUB FAQ.

2. Always mention the information on your GRUB. The version number and the configuration are quite important. If you build it yourself, write the options specified to the configure script and your operating system, including the versions of gcc and binutils.

3. If you have trouble with the installation, inform us of how you installed GRUB. Don't omit error messages, if any. Just 'GRUB hangs up when it boots' is not enough.

   The information on your hardware is also essential. These are especially important: the geometries and the partition tables of your hard disk drives and your BIOS.

4. If GRUB cannot boot your operating system, write down *everything* you see on the screen. Don't paraphrase them, like 'The foo OS crashes with GRUB, even though it can boot with the bar boot loader just fine'. Mention the commands you executed, the messages printed by them, and information on your operating system including the version number.

5. Explain what you wanted to do. It is very useful to know your purpose and your wish, and how GRUB didn't satisfy you.

6. If you can investigate the problem yourself, please do. That will give you and us much more information on the problem. Attaching a patch is even better.

   When you attach a patch, make the patch in unified diff format, and write ChangeLog entries. But, even when you make a patch, don't forget to explain the problem, so that we can understand what your patch is for.

7. Write down anything that you think might be related. Please understand that we often need to reproduce the same problem you encountered in our environment. So your information should be sufficient for us to do the same thing—Don't forget that we cannot see your computer directly. If you are not sure whether to state a fact or leave it out, state it! Reporting too many things is much better than omitting something important.

   If you follow the guideline above, submit a report to the Bug Tracking System. Alternatively, you can submit a report via electronic mail to bug-grub@gnu.org, but we strongly recommend that you use the Bug Tracking System, because e-mail can be passed over easily.

   Once we get your report, we will try to fix the bugs.

Appendix C Where GRUB will go

GRUB 2 is now quite stable and used in many production systems. We are currently working towards a 2.0 release.

If you are interested in the development of GRUB 2, take a look at the homepage.

Appendix D Copying This Manual

D.1 GNU Free Documentation License

Version 1.2, November 2002

Copyright © 2000,2001,2002 Free Software Foundation, Inc.
51 Franklin St, Fifth Floor, Boston, MA 02110-1301, USA

Everyone is permitted to copy and distribute verbatim copies
of this license document, but changing it is not allowed.

0. PREAMBLE

   The purpose of this License is to make a manual, textbook, or other functional and useful document *free* in the sense of freedom: to assure everyone the effective freedom to copy and redistribute it, with or without modifying it, either commercially or non-commercially. Secondarily, this License preserves for the author and publisher a way to get credit for their work, while not being considered responsible for modifications made by others.

   This License is a kind of "copyleft", which means that derivative works of the document must themselves be free in the same sense. It complements the GNU General Public License, which is a copyleft license designed for free software.

   We have designed this License in order to use it for manuals for free software, because free software needs free documentation: a free program should come with manuals providing the same freedoms that the software does. But this License is not limited to software manuals; it can be used for any textual work, regardless of subject matter or whether it is published as a printed book. We recommend this License principally for works whose purpose is instruction or reference.

1. APPLICABILITY AND DEFINITIONS

   This License applies to any manual or other work, in any medium, that contains a notice placed by the copyright holder saying it can be distributed under the terms of this License. Such a notice grants a world-wide, royalty-free license, unlimited in duration, to use that work under the conditions stated herein. The "Document", below, refers to any such manual or work. Any member of the public is a licensee, and is addressed as "you". You accept the license if you copy, modify or distribute the work in a way requiring permission under copyright law.

   A "Modified Version" of the Document means any work containing the Document or a portion of it, either copied verbatim, or with modifications and/or translated into another language.

   A "Secondary Section" is a named appendix or a front-matter section of the Document that deals exclusively with the relationship of the publishers or authors of the Document to the Document's overall subject (or to related matters) and contains nothing that could fall directly within that overall subject. (Thus, if the Document is in part a textbook of mathematics, a Secondary Section may not explain any mathematics.) The relationship could be a matter of historical connection with the subject or with related matters, or of legal, commercial, philosophical, ethical or political position regarding them.

The "Invariant Sections" are certain Secondary Sections whose titles are designated, as being those of Invariant Sections, in the notice that says that the Document is released under this License. If a section does not fit the above definition of Secondary then it is not allowed to be designated as Invariant. The Document may contain zero Invariant Sections. If the Document does not identify any Invariant Sections then there are none.

The "Cover Texts" are certain short passages of text that are listed, as Front-Cover Texts or Back-Cover Texts, in the notice that says that the Document is released under this License. A Front-Cover Text may be at most 5 words, and a Back-Cover Text may be at most 25 words.

A "Transparent" copy of the Document means a machine-readable copy, represented in a format whose specification is available to the general public, that is suitable for revising the document straightforwardly with generic text editors or (for images composed of pixels) generic paint programs or (for drawings) some widely available drawing editor, and that is suitable for input to text formatters or for automatic translation to a variety of formats suitable for input to text formatters. A copy made in an otherwise Transparent file format whose markup, or absence of markup, has been arranged to thwart or discourage subsequent modification by readers is not Transparent. An image format is not Transparent if used for any substantial amount of text. A copy that is not "Transparent" is called "Opaque".

Examples of suitable formats for Transparent copies include plain ASCII without markup, Texinfo input format, LaTeX input format, SGML or XML using a publicly available DTD, and standard-conforming simple HTML, PostScript or PDF designed for human modification. Examples of transparent image formats include PNG, XCF and JPG. Opaque formats include proprietary formats that can be read and edited only by proprietary word processors, SGML or XML for which the DTD and/or processing tools are not generally available, and the machine-generated HTML, PostScript or PDF produced by some word processors for output purposes only.

The "Title Page" means, for a printed book, the title page itself, plus such following pages as are needed to hold, legibly, the material this License requires to appear in the title page. For works in formats which do not have any title page as such, "Title Page" means the text near the most prominent appearance of the work's title, preceding the beginning of the body of the text.

A section "Entitled XYZ" means a named subunit of the Document whose title either is precisely XYZ or contains XYZ in parentheses following text that translates XYZ in another language. (Here XYZ stands for a specific section name mentioned below, such as "Acknowledgements", "Dedications", "Endorsements", or "History".) To "Preserve the Title" of such a section when you modify the Document means that it remains a section "Entitled XYZ" according to this definition.

The Document may include Warranty Disclaimers next to the notice which states that this License applies to the Document. These Warranty Disclaimers are considered to be included by reference in this License, but only as regards disclaiming warranties: any other implication that these Warranty Disclaimers may have is void and has no effect on the meaning of this License.

2. VERBATIM COPYING

You may copy and distribute the Document in any medium, either commercially or noncommercially, provided that this License, the copyright notices, and the license notice saying this License applies to the Document are reproduced in all copies, and that you add no other conditions whatsoever to those of this License. You may not use technical measures to obstruct or control the reading or further copying of the copies you make or distribute. However, you may accept compensation in exchange for copies. If you distribute a large enough number of copies you must also follow the conditions in section 3.

You may also lend copies, under the same conditions stated above, and you may publicly display copies.

3. COPYING IN QUANTITY

If you publish printed copies (or copies in media that commonly have printed covers) of the Document, numbering more than 100, and the Document's license notice requires Cover Texts, you must enclose the copies in covers that carry, clearly and legibly, all these Cover Texts: Front-Cover Texts on the front cover, and Back-Cover Texts on the back cover. Both covers must also clearly and legibly identify you as the publisher of these copies. The front cover must present the full title with all words of the title equally prominent and visible. You may add other material on the covers in addition. Copying with changes limited to the covers, as long as they preserve the title of the Document and satisfy these conditions, can be treated as verbatim copying in other respects.

If the required texts for either cover are too voluminous to fit legibly, you should put the first ones listed (as many as fit reasonably) on the actual cover, and continue the rest onto adjacent pages.

If you publish or distribute Opaque copies of the Document numbering more than 100, you must either include a machine-readable Transparent copy along with each Opaque copy, or state in or with each Opaque copy a computer-network location from which the general network-using public has access to download using public-standard network protocols a complete Transparent copy of the Document, free of added material. If you use the latter option, you must take reasonably prudent steps, when you begin distribution of Opaque copies in quantity, to ensure that this Transparent copy will remain thus accessible at the stated location until at least one year after the last time you distribute an Opaque copy (directly or through your agents or retailers) of that edition to the public.

It is requested, but not required, that you contact the authors of the Document well before redistributing any large number of copies, to give them a chance to provide you with an updated version of the Document.

4. MODIFICATIONS

You may copy and distribute a Modified Version of the Document under the conditions of sections 2 and 3 above, provided that you release the Modified Version under precisely this License, with the Modified Version filling the role of the Document, thus licensing distribution and modification of the Modified Version to whoever possesses a copy of it. In addition, you must do these things in the Modified Version:

A. Use in the Title Page (and on the covers, if any) a title distinct from that of the Document, and from those of previous versions (which should, if there were any, be listed in the History section of the Document). You may use the same title as a previous version if the original publisher of that version gives permission.

B. List on the Title Page, as authors, one or more persons or entities responsible for authorship of the modifications in the Modified Version, together with at least five of the principal authors of the Document (all of its principal authors, if it has fewer than five), unless they release you from this requirement.

C. State on the Title page the name of the publisher of the Modified Version, as the publisher.

D. Preserve all the copyright notices of the Document.

E. Add an appropriate copyright notice for your modifications adjacent to the other copyright notices.

F. Include, immediately after the copyright notices, a license notice giving the public permission to use the Modified Version under the terms of this License, in the form shown in the Addendum below.

G. Preserve in that license notice the full lists of Invariant Sections and required Cover Texts given in the Document's license notice.

H. Include an unaltered copy of this License.

I. Preserve the section Entitled "History", Preserve its Title, and add to it an item stating at least the title, year, new authors, and publisher of the Modified Version as given on the Title Page. If there is no section Entitled "History" in the Document, create one stating the title, year, authors, and publisher of the Document as given on its Title Page, then add an item describing the Modified Version as stated in the previous sentence.

J. Preserve the network location, if any, given in the Document for public access to a Transparent copy of the Document, and likewise the network locations given in the Document for previous versions it was based on. These may be placed in the "History" section. You may omit a network location for a work that was published at least four years before the Document itself, or if the original publisher of the version it refers to gives permission.

K. For any section Entitled "Acknowledgements" or "Dedications", Preserve the Title of the section, and preserve in the section all the substance and tone of each of the contributor acknowledgements and/or dedications given therein.

L. Preserve all the Invariant Sections of the Document, unaltered in their text and in their titles. Section numbers or the equivalent are not considered part of the section titles.

M. Delete any section Entitled "Endorsements". Such a section may not be included in the Modified Version.

N. Do not retitle any existing section to be Entitled "Endorsements" or to conflict in title with any Invariant Section.

O. Preserve any Warranty Disclaimers.

If the Modified Version includes new front-matter sections or appendices that qualify as Secondary Sections and contain no material copied from the Document, you may at your option designate some or all of these sections as invariant. To do this, add their titles to the list of Invariant Sections in the Modified Version's license notice. These titles must be distinct from any other section titles.

You may add a section Entitled "Endorsements", provided it contains nothing but endorsements of your Modified Version by various parties—for example, statements of peer review or that the text has been approved by an organization as the authoritative definition of a standard.

You may add a passage of up to five words as a Front-Cover Text, and a passage of up to 25 words as a Back-Cover Text, to the end of the list of Cover Texts in the Modified Version. Only one passage of Front-Cover Text and one of Back-Cover Text may be added by (or through arrangements made by) any one entity. If the Document already includes a cover text for the same cover, previously added by you or by arrangement made by the same entity you are acting on behalf of, you may not add another; but you may replace the old one, on explicit permission from the previous publisher that added the old one.

The author(s) and publisher(s) of the Document do not by this License give permission to use their names for publicity for or to assert or imply endorsement of any Modified Version.

5. COMBINING DOCUMENTS

You may combine the Document with other documents released under this License, under the terms defined in section 4 above for modified versions, provided that you include in the combination all of the Invariant Sections of all of the original documents, unmodified, and list them all as Invariant Sections of your combined work in its license notice, and that you preserve all their Warranty Disclaimers.

The combined work need only contain one copy of this License, and multiple identical Invariant Sections may be replaced with a single copy. If there are multiple Invariant Sections with the same name but different contents, make the title of each such section unique by adding at the end of it, in parentheses, the name of the original author or publisher of that section if known, or else a unique number. Make the same adjustment to the section titles in the list of Invariant Sections in the license notice of the combined work.

In the combination, you must combine any sections Entitled "History" in the various original documents, forming one section Entitled "History"; likewise combine any sections Entitled "Acknowledgements", and any sections Entitled "Dedications". You must delete all sections Entitled "Endorsements."

6. COLLECTIONS OF DOCUMENTS

You may make a collection consisting of the Document and other documents released under this License, and replace the individual copies of this License in the various documents with a single copy that is included in the collection, provided that you follow the rules of this License for verbatim copying of each of the documents in all other respects.

You may extract a single document from such a collection, and distribute it individually under this License, provided you insert a copy of this License into the extracted document, and follow this License in all other respects regarding verbatim copying of that document.

7. AGGREGATION WITH INDEPENDENT WORKS

A compilation of the Document or its derivatives with other separate and independent documents or works, in or on a volume of a storage or distribution medium, is called an "aggregate" if the copyright resulting from the compilation is not used to limit the legal rights of the compilation's users beyond what the individual works permit. When the Document is included in an aggregate, this License does not apply to the other works in the aggregate which are not themselves derivative works of the Document.

If the Cover Text requirement of section 3 is applicable to these copies of the Document, then if the Document is less than one half of the entire aggregate, the Document's Cover Texts may be placed on covers that bracket the Document within the aggregate, or the electronic equivalent of covers if the Document is in electronic form. Otherwise they must appear on printed covers that bracket the whole aggregate.

8. TRANSLATION

Translation is considered a kind of modification, so you may distribute translations of the Document under the terms of section 4. Replacing Invariant Sections with translations requires special permission from their copyright holders, but you may include translations of some or all Invariant Sections in addition to the original versions of these Invariant Sections. You may include a translation of this License, and all the license notices in the Document, and any Warranty Disclaimers, provided that you also include the original English version of this License and the original versions of those notices and disclaimers. In case of a disagreement between the translation and the original version of this License or a notice or disclaimer, the original version will prevail.

If a section in the Document is Entitled "Acknowledgements", "Dedications", or "History", the requirement (section 4) to Preserve its Title (section 1) will typically require changing the actual title.

9. TERMINATION

You may not copy, modify, sublicense, or distribute the Document except as expressly provided for under this License. Any other attempt to copy, modify, sublicense or distribute the Document is void, and will automatically terminate your rights under this License. However, parties who have received copies, or rights, from you under this License will not have their licenses terminated so long as such parties remain in full compliance.

10. FUTURE REVISIONS OF THIS LICENSE

The Free Software Foundation may publish new, revised versions of the GNU Free Documentation License from time to time. Such new versions will be similar in spirit to the present version, but may differ in detail to address new problems or concerns. See `http://www.gnu.org/copyleft/`.

Each version of the License is given a distinguishing version number. If the Document specifies that a particular numbered version of this License "or any later version" applies to it, you have the option of following the terms and conditions either of that specified version or of any later version that has been published (not as a draft) by the Free Software Foundation. If the Document does not specify a version number of this License, you may choose any version ever published (not as a draft) by the Free Software Foundation.

D.1.1 ADDENDUM: How to use this License for your documents

To use this License in a document you have written, include a copy of the License in the document and put the following copyright and license notices just after the title page:

```
Copyright (C)  year  your name.
Permission is granted to copy, distribute and/or modify this document
under the terms of the GNU Free Documentation License, Version 1.2
or any later version published by the Free Software Foundation;
with no Invariant Sections, no Front-Cover Texts, and no Back-Cover
Texts.  A copy of the license is included in the section entitled ``GNU
Free Documentation License''.
```

If you have Invariant Sections, Front-Cover Texts and Back-Cover Texts, replace the "with...Texts." line with this:

```
with the Invariant Sections being list their titles, with
the Front-Cover Texts being list, and with the Back-Cover Texts
being list.
```

If you have Invariant Sections without Cover Texts, or some other combination of the three, merge those two alternatives to suit the situation.

If your document contains nontrivial examples of program code, we recommend releasing these examples in parallel under your choice of free software license, such as the GNU General Public License, to permit their use in free software.

Index

www.ingramcontent.com/pod-product-compliance
Lightning Source LLC
LaVergne TN
LVHW060144070326
832902LV00018B/2938